Our Part

The Christian Life in Perspective

PAUL ASHLEY

SeeLight
Publishing
Toney, Alabama

Our Part
Copyright © 2013 by Paul Ashley

All rights reserved.

Unless otherwise indicated, Scripture quotations used in this book are taken from the New American Standard Bible, Copyright © 1960, 1962, 1963, 1968, 1971, 1972, 1973, 1975, 1977, 1995 by The Lockman Foundation. Used by permission. (www.Lockman.org)

Scriptures indicated KJV are from The Authorized King James Version.

Scriptures indicated J. B. Phillips are from THE NEW TESTAMENT IN MODERN ENGLISH, Revised Edition by J. B. Phillips. Copyright © 1958, 1960, 1972 by J. B. Phillips. All rights reserved. Reprinted with the permission of Scribner Publishing Group, a part of Simon & Schuster, Inc.

Reprinted by permission. *Living Above the Level of Mediocrity*, Charles Swindoll, 1987, Thomas Nelson Inc., Nashville, Tennessee. All rights reserved.

Reprinted by permission. *When I Relax I Feel Guilty*, Tim Hansel, 1979, David C. Cook Publishing Company, Elgin, Illinois. All rights reserved.

Reprinted by permission. *Perilous Pursuits*, Joseph M. Stowell, 1994, Moody Press, Chicago, Illinois. All rights reserved.

Published by SeeLight Publishing

ISBN: 978-0-9894452-0-7

*This book is lovingly dedicated to Mom and Dad.
The memory of her ever-present praise of our Lord
and
his unwavering faithfulness
will always be with me.
They rejoice in a heavenly home now
and
I look forward with the greatest longing
to see them again someday.*

For with Thee is the fountain of life;
in Thy light we see light.

— PSALMS 36:9

Contents

Introduction 1

1. A Soft Touch 5

2. I Will 17

3. Not a Cake Walk 33

4. All In a Day's Work 59

5. A Relationship Complete 81

6. No Regrets 91

Notes 99

About The Author 103

If you devoted every moment of your whole life exclusively to His service you could not give Him anything that was not in a sense His own already.

— C.S Lewis,
MERE CHRISTIANITY

Introduction

Estimates of population statistics by Operation World reveal that about 2.2 billion people today are labeled as Christians or followers of Christ. This includes dozens of major denominations. Among them there is no more distinguishing trait than the diversity of doctrine regarding man's role in his relationship with God. One would hardly imagine that from the first century days of early Christianity this simple truth would be so difficult to lay hold of and retain considering the effort devoted in the Text to its clear understanding. Yet even among those named as Biblical Christians, this has forever been not only a point of doctrinal contention but more importantly a potential hindrance to the fulfilled life with God.

Just as surely as the Bible teaches that an eternal relationship with God can only begin with a God-centered, grace alone, encounter with the Lord, the same Text also teaches that a fulfilled relationship can only be enlarged and sustained through effort, obedience, and discipline in tune with God's purpose. There are many who have been introduced to and long accepted the truth of the Bible that salvation is secured by first recognizing their own sin and its consequences of eternal separation from God. And then by believing, the sacrificial death and resurrection of Jesus Christ endows a once and for all settlement, a covenant with God never to be broken.

But inseparable with our acknowledgement of Jesus Christ as the Son of God, Creator and Master of the universe, is also our allegiance to Him as the Lord and Master of our lives. Many Christians, ready to recite the first are often reluctant to remember the second. But there can hardly be one without the other. After all, would not the subjects of a beloved king, without reservation, pledge their lives to him.

I hastily add that it is not my intention to be diverted into the debate over lordship salvation. I will let others parse words in that matter. I would only point to the thief on the cross beside Jesus who had little time to consider such doctrinal details. He knew only that the One next to him was indeed the Son of God, that he was indeed a sinner deserving of death, and the Son of God could save him. And if that thief could have come down from his cross, I have no doubt that he would have immediately bowed to the ground as so many others had done, worshiping his King with dedicated allegiance for a lifetime to come.

Each new Christian is like a worn and stained painter's canvas, lovingly set upon the easel, carefully brushed over with the purest white, until no blemish remains. Only then may the skilled master lift his palette, wet his brush, and begin his craft. Now as our Master painter has prepared the canvas of our lives, He desires to complete His masterpiece.

This is a noble hope for the Christian longing to be content and at peace with God, to live a life worthy of His honor, but oh how elusive it can be, particularly today. In this new century, now over a decade old, the world culture has become less distant or distinct. And with it the influence of the culture is pervasive in both subtle and not so subtle ways.

However, one thing has not changed, at least not for the better. That is the ever present pride of man, a man-centered world view. It dominates old and young, leaders and followers, rich and poor, whether it concerns a solution to world peace or how to choose a financial investment to yield the greatest personal wealth and pleasure in the shortest time. Our society is caught up more than ever in materialism instead of morals. Many no longer consider the Bible as a standard of irrefutable instruction. Recent decades have taken their toll. In fact, most could not even detect if it were being misquoted; others do not care. But for those who desire to continue through life's journey dedicated to making every possible day profitable and to ending this life longing to hear, "well done, good and faithful servant", the simple theme of this book is intended to etch into the memory a few compelling thoughts.

It was over a decade ago that I started this book musing that someday I would complete it if the Lord ever granted me the time and its content were not by then long outdated. Well, these many years later it seems no less a prompting within to complete the endeavor. Now having seasoned these few thoughts with the experience of the past years since I began this writing, I have found those same thoughts to act as magnets, attracting common nuggets from verse after verse on almost a daily basis. My hope is that the reader will enlarge his own appreciation of God's guiding hand in their life through these pages.

Paul Ashley, DSc

A Soft Touch

Studies have shown that if your senses are working normally you can feel on your skin the depression made by about 40 millionths of an inch of pressure and that you can see a candle flame thirty miles away on a clear dark night. You can smell one drop of perfume diffused in a three bedroom apartment and you can taste .04 ounces of table salt dissolved in 130 gallons of water. You should be able to feel the weight of a bee's wing falling from less than half of an inch away onto your cheek. You can distinguish from among more than 300,000 different colors and you can gauge the direction of a sound by the difference in arrival times as small as thirty millionths of a second between your two ears.[1] There is certainly no exaggeration in the Bible's declaration that we "are fearfully and wonderfully made".

There is a particularly famous painting by Michelangelo which is found in the Sistine Chapel. He began work on it in 1508 as a fresco, one of many that he completed on the ceiling there. It is called "The Creation of Adam". The scene depicts the likeness of God with his arm outstretched and his hand extended as he reaches toward His creation, while Adam earnestly reaches back toward God to engage the delicate touch of two fingertips. Aside from the artistic liberty taken in the depiction of God and His heaven, it calls to mind the sensitive personal relationship that the Creator originally both planned and desired for us as His children.

In the Bible there are passages which describe not only that relationship but also how God made us. In Genesis 1:26 the Bible tells us that God created us in His own image, even in His own likeness. We find recorded in Psalms 8:5, taking a very literal translation, "You have made man lacking just a little of God in him". Since God put so much of Himself into man, one would expect the same tender and sensitive nature to be evident in His personal relationship with us.

A careful look will reveal a special link to God in His relationship with man. We often call it the conscience. The conscience is as much a part of the way that God relates to our inner person as our senses are to our ability to relate to the outer or physical world and potentially just as sensitive.

Pastor Adrian Rogers once told the story of a homeschool mom who was attempting to instruct her daughter. After some effort the mom decided to evaluate her accomplishments. She began by asking her daughter some questions to review her progress. She inquired, "Do you know the difference between conscious and conscience?" To this the daughter quickly replied, "Sure, mom. Conscious is when we are aware of something and conscience is when we wish we weren't."

There is perhaps more than a little truth there. The word conscience comes from two Latin words, *scire*, which means "to know" and *con* which means "together", combined they mean "to know together". The Greek word, *syneidesis*, that we often find translated "conscience" in the Bible means "co-knowledge" or knowledge of one's self. Further, in the Hebrew Text we also find a word commonly translated conscience. This word, *leb*, is not only translated in the context of conscience but is also the word that is often used, almost 400 times in fact, to depict the heart. It is translated heart many times because the heart is so closely related to the inner mind or inner man which is the root from which this word is derived.

In the Old Testament there are a number of examples which illustrate this connection between the heart and the conscience. When King Saul was pursuing David, the young fugitive found refuge in a cave. While hiding there, Saul came into the cave unknowing of David's presence. David snipped off a small piece of his robe and the Text reads that immediately David's "heart smote him" (1 Samuel 24:5). This term is elsewhere translated, his "conscience bothered him". A similar rendering comes on another occasion in David's life after he numbered the people (2 Samuel 24:10). Immediately afterward he realized the sin against God which he had committed, violating God's specific prohibition. Notice particularly that David's immediate response to this tug on the heart was a recognition of the presence of God.

Linked to the idea of a conscience, as well as the heart which is so much a vital part of it, we see God's connection, His link to us. Just as God fashioned our outward bodily senses, so wonderfully made to be especially sensitive to the world around us, He also made an inner part of us which is intended to be responsive just to Him. There should always be little tender spots in our heart that God can touch very easily, places that He can very easily reach, and that He can speak to without hindrance. I have been often reminded of this as a parent because as dads we tend to have a certain kind of overpowering influence on our children even more so than mom. There is a kind of look you can give your children. All it takes is a steady latching contact with the eyes at any distance. Immediately as eyes are locked there's communication even a hundred yards away. With my children a short pause on their part was often followed by the exclamation, "WHAT?!"

Yes, the conscience is a most peculiar attribute which God has given to us. But I am tempted to issue a warning when I speak of this because there is something that is indeed so unusual about it. It is simply this. Once the conscience is set, it is not easily undone...whether set for good or set for evil. The Bible often speaks of this characteristic of the conscience. We find mention of a weak conscience, a shipwrecked conscience, a seared conscience, a defiled conscience, and an evil conscience. But on the other hand God's Word also speaks of a conscience turned or set toward good and it refers to a clear conscience, a good conscience, and a cleansed conscience. A conscience can be set in a way which responds in a good way or in an evil way. And with this I am undeniably aware and quick to realize that even as my conscience may be set to respond as God would have it, there comes an inevitable change in me.

As I begin to grow more responsive this may even become a bit disconcerting. You see our comfort zone will start to shrink and its boundary seem smaller as God begins to set our conscience ever so sharp and keen. So we must be ready and willing to enter into that kind of tempered growth, accepting the measured change in our lives. We must be willing to accept the discomfort in order to enjoy benefit.

On April 14, 1996, the one year anniversary of the Oklahoma City bombing was remembered. In a TV interview that day a woman who had been a surviving victim of the tragedy was questioned by a reporter. She was across the street in an office building at the time of the bombing and suffered a number of lacerations from flying glass later requiring over 200 stitches. As she spoke she related how the incident had changed her life. She lamented, "I can't do the things I used to do; I'm different inside. I'm not the same, and I want to be the way I was before".

We can readily sympathize with her and imagine what that must be like to have gone through such a unique tragedy and have your life changed by such an event. But you know when God works on us there are events that come into our lives that change us forevermore. They are put there by God in a way which helps us to grow. Therefore, we should expect change and in that sense we should not be afraid to never be as we were before. With advancement some changes are expected. In our newly found condition we are beyond returning to the well worn place of our past.

Consider for a moment the relationship between a child and his or her parents. What a special relationship that is. A small child comes into the world without a care or worry. On the one hand the parent may be described as the one who has all authority over the world of the child and takes care of all provision. The child is completely dependent upon the parent. These overshadowing characteristics become the very nature of the parent's perspective. On the other hand, consider the perspective of the child. He is completely dependent upon the parent and under the authority of the parent. Then as the child grows, there is a certain inherent freedom that the parent begins to relinquish to the child until the time comes when he is released completely. And that emergent freedom slowly, but inevitably, takes on its own special role. But with that freedom comes something else. It's called responsibility. Every parent goes to great lengths to introduce their child to this less coveted partner. But unmistakably, responsibility is intended to grow with them along with their freedom.

The Bible often uses this analogy of the parent and child as an illustration of our relationship with God. We are referred to as the children of God, as the children of a heavenly father. When we consider the attributes just described, we recognize that God is the all encompassing authority and He is the one that provides for all needs. He is the one upon whom the child is fully dependent. However, for the child, which represents the believer, there is a freedom given and he is to grow in that freedom while at the same time recognize the responsibility that goes with it. Here then we have a living picture of what God intended in our relationship with Him. We are insightfully reminded of each part and how they fit together. If we were to remove or disturb any part, it would be as if removing or disturbing that same area in the life of a child and parent. If you take away from his freedom, in reality you take away from what that child may become. Likewise, every parent knows all too well that if the child doesn't accept the responsibility, then the relationship between parent and child will be spoiled. Similarly, the parent is responsible for certain things, for which the child is dependent.

In our relationship with God we don't have to worry about the first part of that relationship. We can count on God there. As for authority, He's all in authority; no doubt there. Dependence? He was concerned about us before the first second ticked off the clock of time in eternity past. As for the child of God, there's a freedom that God gives and there is also a responsibility that goes with it. That becomes the part for which we are to be thoughtfully and intently concerned. Pastor and author A.W. Tozer put it this way,

> Now if God had made us humans to be mere machines we would not have the power of self determination, but since he made us in his own image and made us to be moral creatures he's given us that power of self determination.[2]

Then he goes on to say that even though we have the power of self determination we don't have, as he puts it, "the right of self determination". He writes that God only gave us the right to choose good. He did not give us the right to choose evil even though he gave us the power to do so. And so when we choose evil we usurp the right in order to exercise the power. On the other hand we do not have the power to choose good. We depend fully on God for that. To put it is the simplest terms, although God is wholly needed, we are wholly responsible.

The Bible, as it describes the relationship we have with Him, very clearly illustrates God's part. Over and over we see the magnificence of God in each provision, everything done in order, all brought about with certainty and dependability, totally rendered out of complete love. A love we can hardly imagine or comprehend. But often what happens with believers is that we begin to become confused and overwhelmed about our part. Our misguided self-discipline motivates us to a drill sergeant's routine of chin up, shoulders back, chest out, stomach in...don't breathe... After a few seconds we turn blue and suddenly realize that we can't possibly keep this up. And so the Christian life sometimes degenerates into a lot of do's, don'ts, and don't know how's. The problem is that we often appropriate the characteristics of the Christian life *before* the relationship. The relationship has to come first. Looking to the Bible there are many such illustrations. I have often been reminded of this as part of the struggle that the apostle Paul described in Romans Chapter 7 as he said "For the good that I would, I do not; but the evil which I would not, that I do" (verse 19). But not to leave the struggle without resolution he goes on to say in verse 25 of Chapter 7,

> Thanks be to God for Jesus Christ our Lord so then as on the one hand I myself with my mind serving the law of God but on my other with my flesh the law of sin.

In Christ he was able through his mind to secure the relationship that he knows he should have. Jesus often spoke of the importance of this relationship. He even told his disciples just before he left them that it was actually to their advantage that he leave because it was only then that the spirit of God could come and live inside of them.(John 16:7) That relationship needed completion.

Reflecting back on the lives of the disciples during the time that Jesus was on the earth much of it was a lesson in disappointment. Yet they had Jesus right there in front of them. He was the best example of all the characteristics of a Christian that anyone could ever desire to have. But once he was gone and the spirit of God came to dwell inside of them, that same power working through them accomplished some of the greatest works recorded of man. God's spirit has long worked in the hearts of men. Chapter 11 of Hebrews recounts what is often called the "Hall of Faith". As we scan the list of Old Testament characters found there it is halting to ask, "Were they great in the characteristics they portrayed through their lives or in their relationship with God?" You've got to get the relationship right and it has to grow daily before characteristics take on any meaning. The characteristics will follow if the relationship is healthy and growing on a daily basis.

There is another thing to clearly recognize, however. Indeed there are two sides to the relationship, both God and man. But, it must always be remembered that there is only one side which will ever change. As Tozer so aptly put it,

> In all our efforts to find God, to please him, to commune with him, we must remember that all change must be on our part.[3]

For Malachi 3:6 says, "I am the Lord. I change not."

Now we are ready to ask the question, "What is our part in that relationship?" Let's break it down and see it in the context of what God expects from us aside from all the lofty platitudes. Ponder for a moment aside from the many different ways that we view ourselves and how we're supposed to behave, or as so many would say, the do's and don'ts. Then very clearly and simply we may see our part in that relationship. And in seeing it will grow and mature as we continue to draw nearer and nearer to God. Looking more closely three elements emerge that fit the context of biblical instruction. Being careful to avoid stereotypes, though admitting the risk, three words become our focus. The first is the *"Will"*, the second is the *"Walk"*, and the third is the *"Work"*. Searching past the obvious definitions, we seek to find what God wants in our relationship. As Christians we often ask, "What is it that He really expects of us? What is it that we can do to make our lives satisfying to Him?" Just ahead are some uncomplicated but lucid answers.

I Will

Before considering anything of what you or I would choose to do as an exercise of our will it is always instructive to first recognize the undergirding nature of God's will. In Paul's letter to the Ephesians he writes in Chapter 1, beginning with verse 3 and continuing through verse 12,

> Blessed be the God and Father of our Lord Jesus Christ, who has blessed us with every spiritual blessing in the heavenly places in Christ, just as He chose us in Him before the foundation of the world, that we should be holy and blameless before Him. In love He predestined us to adoption as sons through Jesus Christ to Himself, according to the kind intention of His ***will***, to

the praise of the glory of His grace, which He freely bestowed on us in the Beloved. In Him we have redemption through His blood, the forgiveness of our trespasses, according to the riches of His grace, which He lavished upon us in all wisdom and insight. He made known to us the mystery of His ***will***, according to His kind intention which He purposed in Him with a view to an administration suitable to the fullness of the times, that is, the summing up of all things in Christ, things in the heavens and things upon the earth. In Him also we have obtained an inheritance, having been predestined according to His purpose who works all things after the counsel of His ***will***, to the end that we who were the first to hope in Christ should be to the praise of His glory. In Him, you also, after listening to the message of truth, the gospel of your salvation-- having also believed, you were sealed in Him with the Holy Spirit of promise, who is given as a pledge of our inheritance, with a view to the redemption of God's own possession, to the praise of His glory. (italics mine)

Three times in this passage God's will is specified. We read of the intention of His will, the mystery of His will, and counsel of His will. This part of God's will is totally beyond question and established from eternity past to eternity future. It is often called God's "determined" will. In it we find those things that are totally certain and sure according to God's purpose in this world. Ephesians Chapter 1 is an excellent place for this observation. He planned the lives of every one of us at a time which precedes even our imagination, before time itself. Those plans extend all the way into eternity future. Yet there is another side to God's ever present hand, which is often called His "permissive" will. It comes from the freedom that He has generously given to us. He will not force Himself against that freedom. And it is this second area, the permissive will, that I speak of when I refer to the *Will*.

So what is *our part* related to the *Will*? Well, I have often found that one way of getting at the answer to something of interest is to look at what it is not. One could choose among many passages in scripture to search out the essence of what God wants from us in regard to our will. A very good example is found in Psalms 10. This Psalm represents one particular extreme. Although it doesn't have David's name on it, it is often attributed to him. Psalms 9 and 10 actually fit together. They tell the unenviable story of the wicked. The verses apply one after another to those who obviously do not seek after God. Verse 3 of Chapter 10 says, "For the wicked boast of his heart's desire." And verse 4 continues, "The wicked in the haughtiness of pride (or 'of his countenance' KJV) does not seek him. All his thoughts are there is no God."

As J. Vernon McGee pointed out, there is very little indication that there were many atheists until this time.[1]

David's day and time was much closer to the beginning of man's existence in the world itself. Polytheism, the worship of many gods, was often prevalent and a temptation toward idols was very real even for the people of Israel. But it was very hard to deny the fact that there was a God. Interestingly, we find here that David actually faced people who resisted completely the belief in God. Verse 6 continues, "He hath said in his heart, 'I shall not be moved'."(KJV) Verse 11 uses this same phrase, "He hath said in his heart, God is forgotten"(KJV). Similarly, in verse 13, "He hath said in his heart, thou shalt not require it"(KJV).

Looking at these verses, there are two characteristics of man which stand out clearly. The first is "pride". And connected with it is "heart's desire". So when we consider where the worldly man might place his will, a certain aim stands out. And the direction is revealed by where a person puts his heart's desire. The heart's desire here is shown pridefully toward self. When the heart's desire is turned toward self through pride the will is in the opposite direction from where God wants it to be.

So the will, you see, has to do with where your heart's desire is. And what God seeks is your heart's desire turned toward Him. This is revealed more fully in the passage as we go on a little further. In verse 17 there is a sudden change.

Notice the new paragraph beginning in verse 16 of Psalms 10. Following on, "O Lord thou hast heard the desire of the humble." Pause for a moment to consider by contrast the heart's desire of the humble person, turned toward God. I would be hard pressed for a more appropriate descriptive definition of humility than the one implied here. Humility is a heart turned toward God rather than self. It is indeed the opposite of pride.

What then makes one so presumptuous as to think that the person described here has his heart turned toward God? Looking back one verse the author's deepest sincerity is given away, "The Lord is King forever and ever." It is obvious where his heart lies.

Then what becomes of the person whose heart is turned toward God? In verse 17 we find the answer, "Thou wilt prepare their heart." Interestingly the Hebrew word, "koon" used here for "prepare" or "strengthen" as rendered by some translations, has many complimentary meanings. Both fit together, however, in a way so to imply a list of different attributes associated with the use of the Hebrew word. It carries the figurative meaning "to make ready" or "to erect, to set aright, to perfect, to confirm". It conveys the idea of setting up something. Other meanings include fashioning, fastening firm, framing up, fixing, establishing, ordaining, ordering, and appointing. All of this is contained in the little phrase "prepare their hearts".

That is what God promises for the one whose heart's desire points toward Him, whose will is directed toward Him. That is our part of the will. There are two possible directions, toward self or toward God. That is the choice we make with our will. That is our part. And we make this choice multiple times each day.

So what is the result of a heart prepared by God? The answer is exciting. In a letter to the Roman Christians, the apostle Paul helps to explain. Chapter 2 begins a discourse concerning an age old disparity between Jews and Gentiles. The distinction was often accentuated and complicated more so when placed in the context of the Law. To the Jews the law added to their identity. For the Gentile Christians their place seemed sometimes unclear in relation to the Law. Paul offers an inspiring explanation in this particular passage as he expounds on the relationship with God to which the Gentiles are inseparably joined. Beginning in verse 14,

> For when Gentiles who do not have the Law do instinctively the things of the Law, these, not having the Law are a Law to themselves.

In other words it is written inside of them. Continuing on to verse 15, "in that they show the work of the Law written in their hearts". Still further we read, "their conscience bearing witness, and their thoughts alternately accusing or else defending them". Here is described a distinct role that the conscience plays. You see, when we investigate the heart and the heart's desire, we are not far from the conscience and with it the will of man.

There is something else interesting to be found here. The conscience is said to perform a dual role. The conscience can either move to admonish or it can move to encourage. Both are functions of God's link in His relationship with us. It serves to defend as the apostle Paul often spoke of when he referred to the conscience. He had a "clear conscience". God gave him this ever present strength in his life. But sadly the decline of the conscience in the world today is well confirmed in a book by Ravi Zacharias entitled, *Can Man Live Without God*. In the book he laments the fact that the West has reached a point where it has lost all gratitude for God. And he goes on to say,

> We are living dangerously on this great continent imagining that by our own power, our own will, and our own ingenious capacity we have built history's most modern nation.[2]

It is most ironic to realize that unbelievers generally think that the will is good for something for which God never intended, but on the other hand Christians, often times, behave as if the will is good for nothing. The well known poet, Alfred Lord Tennyson wrote a poem, "In Memoriam", clearly one of his best. He wrote it with much grief as a result of the sudden and unexpected death of a very close friend. Contained therein are these conclusive words,

> Our wills are ours, we know not how.
> Our wills are ours, to make them thine.

That is really what God wants from us, to simply take our will and make it His.

I pause here, digressing slightly, to consider an important aspect of our relationship as well as the attributes of God which have to do with His sovereignty and our own will. Often the idea of God's all encompassing sovereignty tends to get in the way of our concept of the will. Therefore, I wish to clarify this important truth. The height of the Persian Gulf War came near the end of 1990. As the campaign continued swiftly on into January of the next year, the intense planning and purposeful strategy gave way to the decisive military actions of the campaign. Before long initial invasive aerial victories deep within Iraq were won and the United States as well as its allies began to speak of their situation using a term which the media quickly picked up. With each newscast the status of achievement in the conflict was referred to as "supremacy" or "sovereignty" of the skies.

But the true appropriateness of the term could have been justly called into question. Notably, I also recall that we were still compelled to intently continue the attacks upon radar installations as well as any planes or other aircraft that the Iraqis dared place in the skies. And we still appeared to have a great fear of their ground to air missiles as well. The Army even found itself in the uncomfortable position of sending helicopters behind enemy lines to recover downed pilots. That's human sovereignty you see. Human sovereignty always has two clearly distinguished characteristics. It matters not whether it is the Persian Gulf War or any of a number of other world conflicts of the twentieth century. It could be the valiant and honorable efforts of allied nations or just as well a ruthless reign such as the dictatorship of Joseph Stalin or that of Adolf Hitler. The same two characteristics of human sovereignty stand out. First there is always the exercise of power over their enemies or subjects, demonstrated for the purpose of enforcing that sovereignty. Secondly, ever present is a continued fear of the enemy or subjects, in that they may be a threat to that sovereignty. Those two characteristics are always indicative of a human sovereignty.

By contrast, divine sovereignty is not like that at all. And that's why we sometimes have such trouble comprehending man's relationship with God. An example comes to mind. The scene was the splendid royal palace of Pilate as Jesus was brought to stand before him in judgment. Pilate walked in to make his first appearance all attired in royal robe. Powerful Roman soldiers stood on either side. Jesus stood in stark contrast wearing humble dress as He was soon to be beaten, bloodied, and bruised. The representation of all earthly power stood face to face with the representation of God Himself. Never before had such contrast between divine sovereignty and human sovereignty been more clearly but unknowingly displayed.

In John 18:33 Pilate asked "Are you the King of the Jews?" Jesus answered with a question borne of divine sovereignty. He said, "Are you saying this on your own initiative or did others tell you about Me?" He could have called down from heaven thousands of angels. That is what most of us probably would have done. I think I would have been tempted to vaporize Pilate to a crispy piece of charcoal right on the spot. Instead, He didn't raise even a finger or lift His voice in His own defense. Amazingly, He took time to allow Pilate his freedom to make his decision about who He really is. Jesus asked Pilate if he really wanted to know the answer to this question or is this just something that someone else has told him. Only divine sovereignty could with such composure be that bold, changing the focus to Pilate's heart.

John writes further in verse 10 of Chapter 19 to record that Pilate returned to Jesus' presence and asked, "Do you know that I have the authority to release you or the authority to crucify you?" Jesus answered simply, "You would have no authority over me unless it had been given you from above." That again is divine sovereignty!

Near the end of His time here on the earth Jesus came into Jerusalem. Looking out over the beloved city He cried, "O Jerusalem, Jerusalem". Because of the continued rejection of Jesus by so many people his disciples might have desired for Him to call down fire out of the skies to destroy the people but instead He said sadly, "How often I wanted to gather your children together, the way a hen gathers her chicks under her wings, and you were unwilling" (Matthew 23:37) That is divine sovereignty.

On a business trip some time ago I was aboard a plane making its approach for landing at Portland, Oregon. We were about 50 miles out at about 30,000 feet. As is frequently the case in that part of the country, the sky was overcast. From the vantage point of a window seat on the right side of the plane a blanket of white clouds stretched as far as the eye could see. On a clear day it would be possible to see Seattle in the distance and just south from there the beautiful, majestic peak of Mt. Rainer with its snow capped crown. But on this day only the captivating peak of Mt. Rainer stood out alone above the clouds.

God's sovereignty is much like that scene from the window. Man's freedom, like the blanket of clouds that floated by, dominates the view of all the little mountains and hills trying to make their way up, vying for a place of power in the sky. But one majestic peak stands out above the clouds. In fact, not only do the clouds avoid detracting from that grand pinnacle, they actually serve to enhance it for if those clouds weren't there, the visibility of the peak would be muted in a landscape which reached from horizon to horizon. Those free-floating clouds, gliding over the hills beneath provide only the backdrop for that high rising mountain. That's the way our freedom is, our will is, compared to God's sovereignty just as Pilate's royal will confirmed all the more Jesus' sovereignty over the entire cosmos. As the plane finally descended below the clouds on its final approach to the airport, my attention was drawn in the foreground to a large gray hulk, all that remained of Mt. St. Helen. What was once a smoking, billowing mountain trying in vain to push its way up into the sky was now reduced to a burned out relic... so like human sovereignty.

In the Old Testament when the concept of free will is described or applied, a variation of the Hebrew word "nedabah" is generally used. It means "voluntary" or "spontaneous". Furthermore, it is almost exclusively associated with an offering, specifically a free will offering as referred to in the Mosaic Law (e.g. Leviticus 22:18). We have so far seen that the will may be thought of as the freely given heart's desire pointed toward God. Therefore, what God asks is that our heart's desire be considered an offering to Him. Just like the free will offering, voluntary and spontaneous, pointed toward God. That's our part. Indeed, Tennyson's words still ring true, "Our wills are ours to make them thine."

When Moses wrote and proclaimed God's message in Deuteronomy (a word which means the second giving of the law), he gave it to a new generation of people who were coming on the scene. So he concentrated on the fundamentals of the law. In Chapter 5, verse 29, speaking for God he writes, "O that they had such a heart in them that they would fear me and keep all my commandments always." David, whom God called "a man after His own heart," (1 Samuel 12:14) wrote Psalms 40. Verse 8 says, "I delight to do thy will O my God, thy law is written in my heart." Later he gave his last charge to his son Solomon, the young protégé, who was to take over the kingdom which God had given him. Listen to what David said to him:

> As for you, my son Solomon, know the God of
> your father and serve him with a whole heart

and a willing mind for the Lord searches all hearts and understands every intent of the thoughts." (1 Chronicles 28:9)

After this sobering reminder, he adds this insight. "If you seek Him, He will let you find Him." And that short conclusion is the ultimate outcome from "our part" of the will.

Often times I have thought, "O how much easier it would be if God would just place in front of us a big red button and say to us, 'If you want your will to be Mine, just punch the button'." And we would never have to worry about it again. Wouldn't that be neat? We would never again have to entertain an anxious thought about it. But He didn't do that. I cannot fathom all the reasons that He has for His method but I can suggest a few. For you see without that freedom of the will which He has given to us we cannot have a meaningful relationship with Him of the type the Bible describes. The relationship would have no substance. In addition, and perhaps even more importantly, it is through our free will that God gains His glory.

Among the many theme parks at Disneyworld in Orlando is Epcot which is dedicated to human achievement. The center attraction is a 180 foot high geosphere called Spaceship Earth. Through a door near the bottom guests are hustled into a train of open cars on a track that winds its way to the top with the darkness punctuated routinely by animated characters. Traveling through time as it were over the ages until finally arriving in the future one is surrounded by lights and sounds. Near the end of the ride a display screen in each car prompts the riders to divert their attention to a list of interactive questions, providing personal preferences and traits. With the answers to the questions and using a photograph taken at the beginning of the ride, the computerized screen then displays a personalized Jetsons-like scene from the future for each rider. The unlikely caricatures bring a few laughs as we imagine ourselves mechanically placed in this stereotypical life of perfection replete with every innovation. For a few fleeting seconds in this imaginary world all of life is orchestrated and managed, free of care or worry at the touch of a button.

Back outside of Spaceship Earth where the sun shines bright and hot again, where crowds of people press in, where sounds demand attention, and where the aroma of food on a grill beckons our senses, our mind races on to contemplate our busy schedule of sights to see and things to do before the gates close. The short interlude in Spaceship Earth is a tacit reminder that there is no simple button we can push. Day after day we must make the decisions of life, one at a time, each one of us. And we continue to be challenged and tested by God. What He wants for us is to grow in that relationship with Him. We make it possible by remembering our part. The question to ask ourselves is this; do you have that soft spot in your heart, that tender little place known of your conscience, representing your response to the *Will*? It should always be the desire of the heart to have a place which God can approach and easily touch, easily speak to... It is a private line that needs constant loving attention.

Tim Hansel in a book entitled, *When I relax I Feel Guilty* related this little story:

> An Indian was in downtown New York, walking along with his friend who lived in New York City. Suddenly he said, "I hear a cricket."
> "Oh you're crazy!" his friend replied.
> "No, I hear a cricket. I do. I'm sure of it."
> "It's the noon hour. You know there are people bustling around, cars honking, taxis squealing, noises from the city. I'm sure you can't hear it."
> "I'm sure I do." He listened attentively and then he walked to the corner, across the street, and looked all around. Finally on the other corner he found a shrub in a large cement planter. He dug beneath the leaf and found a cricket.
> His friend was duly astonished. But the Indian said "No. my ears are no different from yours. It simply depends on what you're listening to. Here, let me show you."
> He reached into his pocket and pulled out a handful of change—a few quarters, some dimes, nickels, and pennies. And he dropped it on the concrete.

Every head within a block turned.

"You see what I mean?" the Indian said as he began picking up his coins. "It all depends on what you're listening for."[3]

Charles Wesley wrote over 6000 songs. One of them, written in 1749, is not so popularly sung today. It is more of a prayer than a song and portrays particularly well the longing of a heart sensitive to God as the first two stanzas reflect,

> I want a principle within, of watchful Godly fear,
> A sensibility of sin, a pain to feel it near,
> I want the first approach to feel of pride or wrong desire
> To catch the wandering of my will and quench the kindling of the fire
> From thee that I no more may stray, no more thy goodness grieve.
> Grant me the filial awe I pray, the tender conscience give
> Quick as the apple of an eye, O God, my conscience make
> Awake my soul when sin is nigh and keep it still awake.

Not a Cake Walk

Over a 100 years ago the American poet, Ela Wheeler Wilcox, wrote these words:

> One ship drives East and another drives West,
> With the selfsame winds that blow.
> Tis the set of the sails
> And not the gales
> Which tells us the way to go.[1]

Although much of her thinking was not given to sound theology, none the less these compact poetic lines remind us of a simple truth about the creation in which we live. God provides everything for us. In our relationship with Him He provides all the authority and He provides for all the needs that we have. On one side He is that all sufficient part of the relationship but on the other side there is a freedom and a responsibility that joins together consistent with the expectations that God has for us as part of that relationship. He provides the winds that blow. He provides the ship we are on, even the water to sail in. But when it comes to setting the direction He gives us a choice of deciding how to set the sail: either toward Him or toward self (away from Him). Represented by our choice is the desire that we have concerning God, the desire that we have to turn toward Him or to turn toward self. This is once again a description of one aspect of *our part* in that relationship, the *Will*.

Further, there is a connection or a communication link that God provides for us with the heart, an inner communication that He alone provides. We often call it the conscience. With that God is able to reach inside and touch us. He is able to teach us and to speak to us. The sensitivity of that communication link with God depends upon how our relationship with Him grows. As we discover, God can use the conscience to both admonish and to affirm in our relationship as believers. This first element we have identified as the will. Our part is the desire to turn our direction toward Him instead of self, the desire of our heart. But it doesn't stop there. Because God has so much more that He wants to give *to* us, there is more that He asks *of* us.

This brings us to the next element in our relationship which may be identified as the *walk*. But it is far more than the simple term implies as we shall see. Again let's focus on our part. One need not go far or long in their search through the Bible to find a description of the walk. One of the first places you might likely turn is to the book of Ephesians. It is a letter to the church at Ephesus written by the Apostle Paul. Chapter 4 describes the Christian life as a walk. The word walk is used many times throughout the following passage. He writes beginning in verse 1,

> I therefore the prisoner of the Lord beseech you that you walk worthy of the vocation to which you are called with all lowliness and meekness, with longsuffering, forebearing one another in love, endeavoring to keep the unity of the spirit and the bond of peace. There is one body and one Spirit even as you are called in one hope of your calling, one Lord, one faith, one baptism, one God and Father of all who is above all and through all and in you all.

He continues on, describing what we know to be the Christian life as God would have us to emulate Christ. The Book of Ephesians offers an interesting backdrop to our understanding of the walk. It is one of four letters written by Paul from prison toward the end of his life. We know that much earlier in his ministry he had passed through Ephesus. In fact, he spent some considerable time there. It was a special place for him. Considering that the church at Ephesus was likely this letter's first stop, we recognize that its destination was a church which had been nurtured and had grown for some time. It was a mature church. Paul spent as much as three years there as we learn from the story of his third missionary journey in the Book of Acts. So when he wrote to them he spoke as to a group of mature Christians. He spoke at a high spiritual level and chose to share with them very significant truths.

The letter is divided into two parts. The first speaks primarily about the church, not a particular church but the church body. The second part is more individualized and addresses the attributes of the individual believer. The second half of the book, Chapters 4-6, displays this theme in graphic terms. Each chapter adopts a new illustration of the walk of the believer. Chapter 4 speaks of the new man. Chapter 5 describes believers as part of the bride of Christ. Finally, Chapter 6 likens believers to soldiers. Each distinctive description builds upon the preceding one until all together they complete the picture, forming a compelling array of different attributes that God would like to bestow upon the believer.

Looking closer one sees that the blessings of a well adorned believer are not without a requirement. Before any of these attributes or characteristics are attained, there is required a relationship. When Paul addressed the Ephesians, he spoke from experience having already been with them. He spoke to them in terms of these blessings which were to be given to the individual believers. He spoke not only to explain and describe the abundantly blessed Christian but also of the fruit which would result. And he concluded with a reminder of the very empowerment of the Holy Spirit which was to strengthen them. But before he begins this wonderful description, we find here in chapter 4 the identity of what is our part. Verse 22 concludes, "That in reference in your former manner of life, you lay aside the old self (or 'the old man' KJV)." This verse addresses what is asked of the believer in preparation for building the relationship. What is asked is that this old self or this old man be laid aside, put away, discarded, surrendered if you will.

Looking back to verse 17 the example of the Gentiles is given by comparison, "you walk not," or no longer, "just as the Gentiles also walk in the futility of their mind." The passage goes on to explain, speaking of the Gentiles, "they have given themselves over to sensuality for the practice of every kind of impurity with greediness." They are given over to something. They are surrendered to something. And we are not to be given over or surrendered in that way as they are. We are to surrender or put off that very thing, that old nature, that old man, that old self.

That being done, the verse that follows encourages another instruction. Put on the new self or the new man. You see, that is what comes next. Continuing, we read, "which in the likeness of God has been created in righteousness and holiness of the truth." So we learn that God is the one who created the new man or the new self and therefore we should expect that since it is God created, God has to be the one who outfits us. Indeed, He has something special to give to us but He requires something of us first. He requires that we be willing to put away the old man, the old self first. If we are willing to do that, willing to give that up, then He is already prepared to respond. He is ready to put on the new man, the new self onto every believer. So the relationship begins to find its completeness here.

Although God is needed for the putting on of the new man, He will not put on the new man until the old one is surrendered. So it is that we must address our part of the walk. In fact, the very word "walk" used here is the Greek word, *peripateo*, which means to tread all around, to follow, or to be occupied with. It implies something that you are completely enamored with or consumed by and lends itself to the idea of being surrendered to or given to. The very idea of the walk represents what truly dominates us, where we put our thoughts and time and efforts. Therefore, if our "walk" is to be one that has the characteristics and attributes that God would desire for the believer, we need first accept the instruction that is given on its behalf.

To understand the concept of the ***will*** we have examined the opposite in order to see clearly our part. When you consider the will or the desire of the heart, a direction is indicated – the direction in which we are pointed. Because of this it is very easy to differentiate those two alternate directions by looking at two opposites. This time we will do something different. In order to explore the walk and our part in it we look first at what it represents, an experience of life. It has to do with the activities or the characteristics of life. One place to go to find an understanding of the concept is into the lives of some individuals. And the Bible is full of characters in which we are able to find these particular traits. A classic example or story is found in the life of Abraham and so it is there that we will venture first. In Genesis Chapter 22 is found a description of the well known story of Abraham and Isaac. The story begins in verse 1.

> Now it came about that after these things that God tested Abraham and said to him, "Abraham" and he said to Him, "Here am I" and He said, "take now your son, your only son, whom you love, Isaac, and go to the land of Moriah and offer him there as a burnt offering on one of the mountains of which I will tell you".

Abraham responds, taking the belongings that he needs, and together with a couple of servants he and Isaac set out on their trek. It was about a three day journey. On and on they traveled. It is already the picture of one walking, surrendered to God's command. You can possibly imagine much of what is going through Abraham's mind. Knowing what God has told him and then having three days to slowly walk along and ponder the conflicting thoughts of what may be to come. They make their way up from the area around Ber Sheba and then further toward the ridge of mountains that leads up to Mount Moriah. Finally on the third day Abraham sees the place very high up to which God has brought him. At that point with Isaac alone he continues on. The surrendering process had begun three days earlier as Abraham set out toward Mt. Moriah. He had already accepted what God had told him when he set out on the walk.

Now as he approaches the mountain we learn something else. The surrender process has to be done alone. He must leave his servants and the help of others in order to proceed. No one else can do it for us. The process of surrender was not an easy one for Abraham, nor is it for us today. Up to Mt. Moriah Abraham and Isaac had climbed. A few verses further on we read that he made an altar there and spread wood over it. Then he placed Isaac upon the altar as verse 10 records.

> He stretched out his hand and he took the knife to slay his son, but the angel of the Lord called to him from heaven and he said "Abraham, Abraham," and he said "here am I." He said, "do not stretch out your hand."

That very stretching out of the hand represented the final surrender by Abraham. He was willing to release all that he owned, all that he cared about and just at the moment that he did God gave Isaac back to him.

It is interesting to observe in these short verses how many times God affirms Abraham's process of surrender to Him. In verse 12 God explains, "since you have not withheld your son". He says again in verse 16, "Because you have done this thing and have not withheld your son," and finally in verse 18, "Because you have obeyed My voice". Three times He affirmed that Abraham did exactly what He wanted him to do. Notice in this last verse the critical significance given to God's voice. It is the voice of God which is especially important. With it God reaches the soft spot put in our hearts to touch us and teach us and talk to us. It is obvious that Abraham possessed such a place in his heart. He was able to hear God decisively as He told him what He wanted him to do with Isaac, without question or misunderstanding. Abraham did not say "I don't understand You; surely that's not what You mean." The Text leaves us with no doubt that it was without confusion concerning what God asked Abraham to do. Because his heart was so sensitive, he could hear it clearly. There was also no room for excuse. He could not say later, "I didn't quite understand."

Most of all He was able to hear the voice of God very easily and quickly. Nothing less would do when there were only seconds left to spare Isaac's life. God didn't have to worry about Abraham hearing Him in time. He knew Abraham. And so God said, "Because you have obeyed My voice," heard it and obeyed it, "...all the nations of the earth shall be blessed."

Twice we see in this passage that a blessing is spoken of. It is a blessing which includes not only both Abraham's son and his family but it goes on for innumerable generations to come. In fact, when considering the names of famous people throughout all of history it is hard to imagine anyone whose name is more known the world over in civilized cultures than that of Abraham. Your list may include presidents, statesmen, writers, military leaders, wealthy or influential people, but from the ranks of humankind if you were to inquire of almost anyone in the world within modern civilization it is likely they would know of this man, Abraham. Further, beyond the obvious blessing described, there was an outcome or consequence which resulted from Abraham's obedience to God. In verse 14, we read that "it will be provided". The very name of the place is called Jehovah Jirah, meaning the Lord will provide. It is a provision that is given as a result of this obedience, as a result of his surrender to God. And that same type of God given provision is a blessing that He has for us as a result. It rests in the completion of the relationship that He desires to have with us.

So as we surrender to God there awaits already something special that He has prepared and is ready to give to us. It is that provision that results only from the full surrender in our lives. The word "provide" here comes from the Hebrew word, *raah*, which literally means "to see". It actually carries the meaning of "to see to it", very specifically to take care of something. Without any doubt, without any question God will see to it. And so His provision is certain as a result of our complete surrender.

Not only do we have the assurance of God's action but the Hebrew word is also synonymous with the noun form which was used to mean a bird of prey because of their keen eyesight. This conveys the idea that the very characteristic of that gracious provision is the keen perception of exactly what we need. It is already there waiting to satisfy our need, waiting for our surrender. Remember the ram in the thicket, already there waiting, for just the time when it was needed.

When Jesus addressed the crowds near the shore of Lake Galilee during His well remembered Sermon on the Mount, the very first thing said as recorded in the beatitudes of Matthew chapter 5 was, "Blessed are the poor in spirit for theirs is the kingdom of heaven." To the people of that day the word "poor" would carry the meaning of a beggar on the street, one who was completely dependent in the public domain, one who had nothing, no sustenance, no sufficiency, totally broken, totally surrendered and reliant. When we consider the poor in spirit then, we should be reminded of being totally dependent, totally without our own sufficiency, totally surrendered when it comes to our spirit. And what is the result? The kingdom of God. The unlimited rich blessings of all of God's kingdom await as a provision for those whose sufficiency rests in Him through our surrender. That is what it requires on our part – complete, uncompromising surrender just as it did with Abraham. Indeed, what we find is that those with nothing of their own are actually given everything they need for sufficiency with unimaginable blessings besides.

Another character in the Text illustrative of this same concept is Abraham's grandson. Jacob is indeed a considerable contrast to Abraham. As this adventuresome story beginning in Genesis 25 unfolds, Jacob's early life is fraught with deceit while he sought on his own to acquire possessions. He usurped Esau's birthright. He later matched wits with his Uncle Laban.

Notwithstanding, Laban was at times a pretty good match for him when it came to flocks, herds and wives. As Jacob lived out that early part of his life, his was not one of admirable surrender. But there came a time when God spoke to him and told him to go back to Bethel, back to the place of his home. He acquiesced, being as it were, pursued on one side by Laban and fearful of what faced him on the other with Esau. He was caught reluctantly and quite literally in between a rock and hard place. Just before he reached Esau and his men he was already devising a plan. Perhaps scheming is a better description. He was not really waiting on God but arranging so as to better his situation, fearful of what Esau might do to him. Craftily he parceled out small groups of envoys with gifts, one after another hoping that they would pacify Esau before he arrived. His mind was filled with conniving musings, not trusting that God was the one who had directed him on his journey and that God would provide for him. He was not really surrendered, not given to God's plan for his life. But God had a blessing waiting for him anyway if he would only proceed in the way God wanted.

During the coming night Jacob fought with God as recorded in Genesis 32; all night long he wrestled with Him, holding on, wanting a blessing and not willing to give up, but still not truly surrendered. Not until the end of that long battle does verse 32 read, "The Angel of God said, 'What is thy name?'". That's an interesting question. Why did He ask Jacob his name? Surely He knew. Over 20 years before someone else had asked Jacob, "What's your name?" And determined to deceive he replied, "Esau". This time God wanted to know if he had changed. He wanted to know if he had actually surrendered this time. Was he ready for God to take over and control his life? Finally, overcome with exhaustion, he answered, "Jacob" which means "deceiver".

That was for him the true beginning of his surrender. And then God proclaimed the blessing of a great nation. His name is now "Israel", representing all the blessings that God had for Jacob, a whole nation, an incredible blessing just for him, upon his full surrender. The provision was graciously prearranged and waiting.

I still recall when I was a young child, about 8 or 10 years old, the many household chores in our family. Everyone had different chores that they were to do on a regular basis. Mine included cleaning the bathroom and trimming around the edge of the lawn. Now, back then we did not have weed eaters, so the grass trimming was done with little hand clippers – not a pleasant task. I also had the job of taking out the trash. Of all those chores the one for which I was chastened the most for neglect was not the cleaning of the bathroom nor was it trimming the grass. It was taking out the trash. It was an easy enough chore but I was prone to procrastination. All I had to do was to go around the house from room to room, gather up the trash, put it into a big bag, and carry it out to a container along the fence in the back yard to be picked up once a week. But I was nagged relentlessly.

When I grew up I ended up with the same job, until my oldest son was up to the task at which time this chore was happily passed off to him. At that time in our young family trash collection in our neighborhood came on Tuesdays. That was known as "trash day" around our house. In fact, in order to remember each week I generally associated Tuesday with trash day. I believe that if I were playing a word association game and someone said Tuesday, I would say "trash day".

On that day the process commenced of gathering up all the trash to place in extra big bags (since local trash service has a five bag limit!). So with our now growing family we were sure to use the large 30 gallon trash bags and try to see how much trash can be stuffed into a trash bag before the sides burst. Then with the bag more than safely full, the top of the bag was pulled tightly together just long enough to lasso it with a small plastic tie before standing back with bated breath hoping that it did not languidly slip off. Thanks to modern innovation there are now new bags with handle ties. It is amazing how much trash can be stuffed into those bags and still pull the top closed. But next came the challenge of transporting all the bags to the edge of the road. We had a long driveway. All the trash bags would usually end up in the back of the car with the trunk lid open, flopping up and down methodically. I would then go bouncing down the driveway to set the bags of trash on the side of the road for pick up on Tuesday morning.

I can remember many of those days struggling mirthlessly with the trash and setting it out with the confidence that for my dutiful efforts the trash collector would soon come by that day to pick up the trash; it would be taken, gone, buried, and never seen again. Coming home from work on Tuesday evening I would pull into the driveway, glance over, and assure myself with a certain satisfaction that the trash was actually gone (glad that I had just managed to get it out early enough not to miss the pickup as I was sometimes prone to do).

Why such a long story? Because for me there was an inexplicable feeling of relief to know that the trash was gone. Or maybe for you it is the smile which stirs from seeing years of your accumulated "junk" in the back of *someone else's* car as it drives away from a long overdue yard sale. Well that is sort of the way it is in our relationship with God. There are a lot of things in our lives that we need to surrender. We have to go inside our spiritual house, look in every room, pull out the trash, stuff it into some bags, and then we must set it on the side of the road to let God pick it up, bury it, and never see it again. What He asks of us is that we put it on the side of the road. I've never known a trash collector to back his truck up to the front door and go in to pick up the trash. You must let the collector know what you are going to throw away by setting it on the curb. He will only pick up what's on the curb. And that is the way it is with God.

We have many things that we can hold onto inside of us but unless we reach inside, put them in a bag, set them on the curb, and say I surrender this, they won't get picked up, they won't get buried. In fact we even have an advantage that God will do one more thing for us. He will do what no trash collector will do. He will come inside our hearts and He'll start pointing at things if we will let Him. He'll show us where the trash is. He'll show us what needs to be surrendered if we will let Him do it. And you know everybody has something different that needs to be surrendered.

I remember driving down the road on Tuesday morning only to see everyone else's trash out there on the side of the road too, all different colors... green bags, brown bags, white bags. Some people had cans; some people had boxes. Some families had wheels on their cans so they could get it out to the curb easily. Yes, everyone has something different that they need to surrender, something different inside their trash bag. And each of us has that same responsibility to take it out to the curb and let God pick it up. That's what surrender is all about.

I also remember some time ago that I was going through that little process on Tuesday morning, packing all that stuff into the trash bag like a zealous human compactor until I felt something hard. I reached down inside and under some paper I pulled out a serving spoon. It was a big stainless steel serving spoon. It was part of our matched regular dinnerware set. I pulled it out with growing indignation, waved it up in the air, and cornered the first person in the family I could find to criticize for being so negligent as to leave a spoon in the trash. Another item unsuspectingly found during a trash gathering ritual was a pair of well worn (some would say worn out) work shoes. Of course most in my family would agree this belonged in the trash, but these were very comfortable work shoes. I loved to wear these work shoes although I will admit their life had been extended two or three times over and they have a little extra ventilation on the sides. I had pulled those things out of the trash at least three times following the deliberate, albeit stealthy, maneuver of some well meaning family members.

I can imagine what it must sometimes look like to God when we go around waving our stainless steel serving spoon and wearing our frayed leather shoes while what He would like to put in our hands and cover our feet with are blessings that we cannot even count.

That's what God asks from us. He asks for us to put off the old man. Our part is the surrender. And just like that trash that keeps building up, when gotten rid of, we will make room for the provision that God has for us. But you know, for many of us what we have talked about so far is not always the hard part. I don't have any trouble finding stuff to put in those trash bags. My problem is the five bag limit. We often joke around our house that we occasionally need to bring in a big front end loader to just come and take two or three loads out of the house, to reduce some of the never ending clutter. No, the problem is not so much identifying plenty of trash that we can readily surrender in our lives. And by the way, most of us would hardly miss it. Although at the time we might be fond of keeping those old shoes.

What is the problem then? Well it becomes a little bit clearer by going back for a second look at the illustration of Abraham. There we find the core of a real conflict. What bothered Abraham was not that he had some trash that needed throwing out. It was that he had something of great intrinsic value. What a conflict this was. Isaac was certainly not what anyone would consider trash. He was of great value, a human being, part of the family. In addition, Isaac represented the blessing for all of his future. God had promised it to him. The conflict there you see, the surrender, was a hard one because of what had to be surrendered.

This is a case where it helps to know the end of the story. For it is then that God's intent is discerned. It was not Isaac that was ultimately to be surrendered or done away with. But rather it was the *possession* and *ownership* of him. And that is the hard part. God has brought many things into our lives which He has placed there, providentially planned as part of a provision or blessing. However the possession of it, the ownership of it, is not ours to have and we must surrender it. That is what Abraham had to come to terms with. Abraham knew Isaac was part of the plan. He knew he had to have a son. He knew this was part of his blessing. He knew if God took Isaac, another provision would be made. Abraham fully expected to return with Isaac, resurrected if need be as can be seen from verse 5 of Genesis Chapter 22. Isaac was not the problem. The question of God to Abraham really was, "Do you own and possess him or do I?" That was the question he faced and struggled with, as do we. That's **our part** of the **walk** or surrender in our relationship with God.

We have many things that we "possess and own". We have financial security. We have positions and expected opportunities. We have family and children. We have a future filled with our own ambition and anticipation. We have all that we look to or expect in life. God says you cannot own it. You cannot possess it. We are called to give it up. As when Abraham was willing to give up Isaac, then he received God's greatest blessing. Recall God's words again, "because you have done this thing…indeed I will greatly bless you."(Genesis 22:16,17) For him would come generations beyond his greatest imagination.

God's blessings are packaged in advance waiting as a provision of surrender. When Abraham possessed nothing, he indeed had everything. Our lives are no different. Philippians 2:7 speaks of Christ as He came into this world. He is described as having emptied Himself. What did He empty Himself of? It wasn't His deity. He was as much God as He was Man. No, He emptied Himself from the prerogatives of that deity. He gave up all of the privileges, all of those things that He could have had and done to make Himself comfortable. The sound of His voice could beckon angels. Instead He chose the role of a man and lifted His voice to His Father's bidding in His life here on earth. He gave up His visible glory with all its majesty to live as a human being. He emptied Himself to make a space for what God the Father purposed to do in his life. You see that is the reason that surrender is so important.

In our relationship with God there is a space designed especially for Him to fill. He cannot fill it if it's already full, if it is already cluttered. Every time we fail to surrender something we subtract from that space the room needed for His blessing. Jesus emptied Himself fully in order that He received that full blessing and purpose in His life. He is the perfect example of what we are to do.

The ***will*** represents our part in a ***desire toward*** God. Often it is an experience of exhilaration and joy and praise to turn your heart fully toward God, to be directed toward Him and not toward self. It wells up inside soon to overflow. By contrast the ***walk*** is quite different. When we talk about surrender, we are usually talking about something that is bittersweet, something that is often painful but it yields the great blessing of God's provision. It is a process that we must go through and our part is the ***surrender***. So there is really a difference between these two, the ***will*** and the ***walk***. It is genuinely worth recognizing this difference because when you strive to establish those little soft spots in your heart that only God can touch, they will be easily distinguished one from the other. When God wants to touch you, He can reach the heart with no trouble, without confusion, without misunderstanding. When He touches one particular little place, then you know that He is interested in the desire of your heart. When He touches another little spot, you know He is encouraging some surrender in your life. By separating these two we begin to see the difference and recognize what is required, which is our part in those areas of our lives.

Similarly the *will*, as we have seen, is much like an offering to God. The same words are used in the Bible as a freewill offering, something that is given voluntarily, fully, joyfully. Now the *walk* is a little different. It is more like a sacrifice. In fact it goes beyond the desire of the heart to actually giving up the very thing that you hold on to. That is a sacrifice. When Abraham walked up on top of the altar and laid Isaac there, that was a sacrifice. It hurt. And that is the way the walk is. It hurts a little or perhaps a lot to do it. But the blessing is marvelous as He fills back the space. There are actually progressive steps to surrender.

This I have found in my life personally and I have found it to be similarly affirmed in the lives of others as well. It is a three part process. The first starts out with just simply holding on to things that are not really surrendered very well at all. We have a lot of possessions but would prefer not to think of them as such. Then the next step is one in which God may take things from us. In the process we will eventually reach the point of letting Him take it but we stop short of bringing ourselves to the point of offering it to Him very freely. In other words, I may no longer be bitter or resentful if He decides to take it. But the third phase comes when we are really fully surrendered. We don't even wait for God to ask. It is already laid out at arm's reach as we ask first what He wants us to do with it instead of waiting for Him to extract it from our closed fingers. When we get to that point as Abraham did with arms outstretched, when we have reached that level of surrender when God truly owns not only our possessions but every possessive thought and emotion as well, then ***our part*** of the walk is finally complete.

Some years ago Chuck Swindoll wrote a small volume, called *Intimacy with the Almighty*. It surveyed the wisdom of 30 years in the ministry as he looked back and reflected on his life. As he did so, he distilled many of the things that he had learned over that period of time. He outlined, as he saw it, the relationship with God by highlighting the essentials of the growth process which leads there. He presented four disciplines and he progressively advanced from one to the other until finally he reached the fourth and final one. That final one was...surrender. He testifies, "Surrender is the key that unlocks the vault of God's best and deepest treasures." Then he closes the little book with this comment. He said, "I am finally learning that surrendering to my sovereign Lord leaving the details of my future in his hands is the most responsible act of obedience I can do."[2]

In another of his books, *Living Above the Level of Mediocrity*, on the subject of excellence in the Christian life, Chuck Swindoll relates an indelible illustration of the test of true surrender. It is the story of a man who was lost in the desert, dying of thirst:

> He stumbled upon an old shack—a ramshackled, windowless, roofless, weatherbeaten old

shack. He looked about this place and found a little shade from the heat of the desert sun. As he glanced around he saw a pump about fifteen feet away—an old, rusty water pump. He stumbled over to it, grabbed the handle, and began to pump up and down, up and down. Nothing came out.

Disappointed, he staggered back. He noticed off to the side an old jug. He looked at it, wiped away the dirt and dust, and read a message that said, "You have to prime the pump with all the water in this jug, my friend. P.S.: Be sure you fill the jug again before you leave."

He popped the cork out of the jug and sure enough, there was water. It was almost full of water! Suddenly, he was faced with a decision. If he drank the water, he could live. Ah, but if he poured all the water into the old rusty pump, maybe it would yield fresh, cool water from down deep in the well, all the water he wanted.

He studied the possibility of both options. What should he do, pour it into the old pump and take a chance on fresh, cool water or drink what was in the old jug and ignore its message? Should he waste all the water on the hopes of those flimsy instructions written, no telling how long ago?

Reluctantly he poured all the water into the pump. Then he grabbed the handle and began to pump... squeak, squeak, squeak. Still nothing came out! Squeak, squeak, squeak. A little bit began to dribble out, then a small stream, and finally it gushed! To his relief fresh, cool water poured out of the rusty pump. Eagerly, he filled the jug and drank from it. He filled it another time and once again drank from its refreshing contents.

Then he filled the jug for the next traveler. He filled it to the top, popped the cork back on, and added this little note: "Believe me, it really works.

You have to give it all away before you can get *anything* back."[3]

That is the secret of surrender. That is the secret of **our part** in the Christian **walk**. If you want from God all the blessings that He has ready for you, all of those attributes of a fulfilled life in harmony with God such as is described in the Apostle Paul's letter to the Ephesians, you must first make room. If you truly desire all those great things that He wants for us, the abundance that He would like to give us, you must surrender the old man. Then you will have room for His thirst quenching provision.

Jim Elliot, a well known missionary in the 1940's and 50's, graduated from college determined that he was ready to accept God's calling to the mission field. As he sought God's guidance, he ended up in South America, working to break through the language barrier and reach the Auca Indians in Ecuador, Indians known to be very hostile and dangerous. He eventually gave up his life to that cause along with four other missionaries. At the age of about 21 he had begun to write regularly in a journal.

In 1948 he penned this entry, "God, I pray thee, light these idle sticks of my life and may I burn for thee. Consume my life my God. It is thine. I seek not a long life, but a full one, like you, Lord Jesus."[4] And not long after that at the age of 22, he wrote another little entry in his journal. It read, "He is no fool who gives what he cannot keep to gain what he cannot lose."[5] Less than six years later he gave, readily sacrificed, what he had already freely surrendered. That is the way God wants our lives to be, already surrendered, already given, ready for the provision he has for our life, whatever it may be, even if it is a sacrifice.

Ephesians 5:8 tells us that the walk is something that is associated with light. In fact it says, "Walk as children of the light." Because when you empty yourself, completely surrendered, you get all of the "stuff" out of your life and there is a lot of room for light. It just gets kind of airy and light inside. God's light begins to shine through. In his book, *The Pursuit of God*, A. W. Tozer prayed regarding surrender in his life,

> Then shall my heart have no need of the sun to shine in it, for thy self will be the light of it and there shall be no night there.[6]

All In a Day's Work

Joseph Stowell, former president of Moody Bible Institute, related in his book, *Perilous Pursuits*,[1] his experience of visiting the family of one of his students while on a trip to the former Soviet Union. He discovered, to his surprise that he was one of the first foreign visitors to the remote town in 38 years. In this back area of the country he went into the home of the student and his family. While there he also met the pastor of the local church.

Pastor Ivan told the story of his life experience going back many years recalling the troubled and oppressed history dominated by the Soviet ruler Joseph Stalin. He was a young minister at the time. Pastor Ivan described an occasion when the intimidating Soviet secret police of the KGB came to persuade him to report on his congregation while he was still the pastor there. They told him that they would take good care of him and would provide for him if he would be accommodating. He knew that it could mean safety and security for his family. But he looked back at them and said, "No, I cannot do that to my Lord and my people." He knew that such a response would certainly secure for himself a ticket to a Siberian labor camp. And that is exactly what happened. He was soon arrested and sent on his way with 1500 other prisoners aboard a ship in which 600 died in a boiler explosion during the voyage. They were then put to a forced march across the windswept frozen tundra of the Siberian wilderness. Most of their shoe leather was worn off by the time they arrived.

Ivan spent 10 years in the labor camp. He was asked if there were any other Christians there. He replied, "Yes, we would get together often to read the Word to one another, encourage one another, and sing hymns of praise to God." Then he told of a time near the end of his imprisonment in which they would be sent out over a 60 mile radius in the wilderness to build and establish new towns for Stalin. He paused with joy and said, "You know, today there are literally hundreds of churches all over Siberia as a result of those fellowship groups of Christians during those ruthless years of the oppression."

Taken in by the providence of such an experience and the certainty of God's purpose Joe Stowell commented on Ivan's response, "It was as though God in His desire to establish outposts in the Siberian wilderness said to Stalin... 'Take some of my finest servants, those who are not addicted to their significance but to my work, and send them as missionaries to Siberia. And you pay the bill!'" The irony is amplified by the recollection of Stalin's daughter who once told the story of his last days as he lay dying, bedridden, unconscious but for brief moments. On one occasion as she watched, he sat up suddenly in bed and shook his fist at God before finally slipping back into eternity as death overtook him.

We often find as we look at the work of God, the confirmation that he seeks a relationship with us which is wholly complete but also uncompromising. When He finally acquires that from us, it is then that He is able to perform His work in us. We have looked at three different parts of that relationship, breaking it down into three elements – the "will", the "walk" and the "work". The *will* is the desire of the heart as the Bible describes it. That is our part. As a result God prepares our heart and then begins to bestow His immeasurable blessing. The *walk* represents our part in full surrender to God. The result is a complete and lasting provision. Through each of these elements He touches us and is able to speak to us through our growing sensitivity to His voice. We would soon recognize, however, that these two elements are not all that God intends for our relationship with Him. It is not quite complete. There remains another element. The desire of the heart and the surrender to Him merely put us in a most favorable position for the final element of our part...the *work*. And as might be expected there is a part of the work which is our response to Him.

Previously we have examined a diversity of illustrative scriptures in order to search out our part in each element of our relationship with God. Again it is instructive to choose a letter of the Apostle Paul to one of the early churches. But unlike the last letter chosen to the church at Ephesus, a strong church, this time we will chose a different letter and for a different reason. By comparison let us now consider a weak, less mature church, the church at Corinth. The illustration is clear when we look at the first letter Paul wrote to the church. It portrays the way the world looks at things, the way the world thinks. We are then able to see by stark contrast the difference between this earthbound vista and the selfless perspective of the Christian life together with our heaven bound relationship to God.

The Apostle Paul's letter reveals to us the way that the world looks at things. Using the description of the Corinthian church as an example, he contrasts this worldly vision of which we may be prone to have also. And if we view through worldly eyes, we are likewise led to worldly thinking. In so doing you will not see the Christian life as it is meant to be seen. Furthermore, your relationship with God will miss the mark.

Coming to Chapter 3 of 1 Corinthians we arrive at a suitable point of departure. With the first verse the Apostle Paul articulates the weakness to be found very explicitly in the church at Corinth. He says, "And brethren, I could not speak to you as spiritual men but as of to men of flesh and as babes in Christ." "I give you milk to drink," he says in the next verse. As immature Christians he finds that he must relate to them in this manner. He instructs them in fundamentals. He wants them to understand in a way that helps them to draw a contrast to the way the world thinks and the way they too are accustomed to seeing. And this is not unlike the reasoning of so many Christians in the world today.

Paul discusses a particularly disturbing situation in the Corinthian church which had come to his attention. Members of the body had become attracted to certain leaders in the church to the point of exclusive, loyal attachments. Paul recognized it as the influence of a world centered reasoning. Far beyond their affinity for popular human leaders was the affect on their relationships with others in the body and ultimately their relationship with God. He carefully explains his concern and then goes on to correct them in verse 5, "What then is Apollos and what is Paul, servants [or ministers] through whom you believed even as the Lord gave opportunity to each one." He continues on in verses 6-9 to say,

> I planted, Apollos watered, but God was causing the growth. So then neither the one who plants nor the one who waters is anything but God who causes the growth. [or the increase] Now he who plants and he who waters are one but each will receive his own reward according to his own labor. For we are God's fellow workers, we are God's field, God's building.

Notice here in verse 6 and 7 that it is God who causes the growth. It is God who is responsible for the increase or the accomplishment. Look carefully and you will also notice something else in perfect contrast. You will find our part. The J.B. Phillips Bible expresses it well. Back to verse 7 and 8 it says,

> The planter and the waterer are nothing compared to Him who gives life to the seed. The planter and waterer are alike insignificant though each shall be rewarded according to his particular work.

We are certainly very insignificant compared to God. He is the one who provides the accomplishment. This is a suitable lesson for the Corinthians. But the final half of the verse reveals much more. Do not miss it. God cared enough to share with us how important is the special part we have. There is even a reward planned personally by God for it. Although small compared to God's work, it is important enough to Him that a reward awaits such effort. It is truly special to God. Recognizing that God has a special place for our effort proceed a little further down to verse 9 and we see that not only is our effort special, with a unique role for us to play, but He says that we are His "fellow workers"; we are His "laborers together". We are actually to be side by side with Him in every effort that He undertakes with us. Indeed God has reserved a place for us in the work. Continuing in verse 11 Paul explains that the "building" representing the worker's efforts has a peculiar foundation. It is Jesus Christ. We are to be part of the whole work of Jesus Christ, actually part of the building that He is even now constructing on that foundation.

Chapter 4 begins with an instruction to ministers. In verse 1 he speaks to ministers as to leaders of the church but similarly to all in the sense of our ministry in the church. He says, "Let a man regard us in this manner as servants [or ministers] of Christ and stewards of the mysteries of God." Imagine that. Of the very mysteries that God has purposed to reveal we are to be the stewards who preserve and proclaim. We are to be the ministers. We are to be the servants that help in distributing God's revelation to the world. In verse 2 he exhorts, "In this case moreover, watch out. It is required of stewards [that's us] that one be found *trustworthy*"(italics mine). This is a very interesting word. The KJV translates trustworthy as "faithful". The Greek word, *pistos*, has a very definitive meaning, to rely on or to be confident in. Specifically, it can mean sure or true. It is without question a powerful word.

To gather the impact of this meaning and to understand what the Apostle Paul intended when he chose this word, we need not leave the letter of 1 Corinthians. For we can see elsewhere in the letter how the word is used in the context of what exemplified such a steward. Here in 1 Corinthians 1:8 is a description of the promise that God makes of Jesus Christ, given to us, "God is faithful through whom you were called into fellowship with the Son Jesus Christ our Lord." This same word describes the faithfulness of God.

In describing the promise that God makes regarding our protection from temptation, 1 Corinthians 10:13 says, "And God is faithful who will not allow you to be tempted beyond that which you are able." Again God's perfect faithfulness is described with this word. The very same standard that God holds Himself in regard to faithfulness we are to strive for and be responsible unto as stewards in our labors with Him. That is how we are to measure ourselves, the same standard that God sets for Himself, complete faithfulness.

At this juncture it is perhaps easier to see what work is not. Work is not a short task that is soon done. It requires a faithful diligent effort. It is a building process. It is not servile work or forced labor. Fellow workers, stewards with God it is called. Instead the work is an occupation, a long labor, a work of the heart. This phrase, by the way, is similar to that used to describe one Bible character in particular. The verse reads, "In every work which he began in the service of the house of God in law and in commandment seeking his God he did with all his heart and prospered." Do you know who it was? 2 Kings 18:5 records, "He trusted in the Lord, the God of Israel so that after him there was none like him among all the kings of Judah or among those who were before him." It was Hezekiah, the favored king of Judah. The verse just before says, "He removed the high places, he broke down the sacred pillars, he cut down the Asherah." We are even told that he had the courage to take down and break into pieces the bronze serpent that Moses had made because the people had begun to worship it.

The Bible tells us that Hezekiah was a diligent person who was always active doing something. It tells us later that he built treasuries and storehouses in cities and he even built a solid stone tunnel through the rock underneath Jerusalem to bring in water in times of danger. He was always busy and he was busy with things in which the Bible says God prospered him. In fact, later in verse 7 it says wherever he went he prospered. What was it that made Hezekiah so prospered by God in his effort? For one thing he was very diligent in his effort.

The Bible describes here in much detail the activities in which he was involved. But it is often interesting and especially enlightening to find an amplified view of God's perspective by examining the record of the Chronicles in addition to the Kings. As the book of the Kings is a record of the historical Israel, the Chronicles is more a spiritual commentary, God's commentary. We find the same story in 2 Chronicles 31. Verse 20 records the activities of Hezekiah with this comment, "And thus Hezekiah did throughout all of Judah and he did what was good and right and true before the Lord his God." The Greek translation from the Hebrew uses the same word here for true as that used for faithful or trustworthy. For that is how Hezekiah was known. God knew that He could count on him.

There is one particular narration involving Hezekiah, which is recited multiple times in the Text, more than any other in all the history of Israel. This should get our attention. God must want to make sure we get the point. The Assyrians surrounded Jerusalem, placing it under siege during the reign of Hezekiah. He was placed in a hopeless predicament and as the event unfolded, it is recorded in 2 Chronicles. It is also recorded in the records of the Kings as well as in Isaiah. Three times the same story is told. Just one chapter later (Chapter 32 of 2 Chronicles) we find the words that Hezekiah gave to the people, "for the one with us is greater than the one with him. With him is only an arm of flesh but with us is the Lord our God to help us to fight our battles."

You see Hezekiah understood something about the way the world thinks. A Godless world expects all that is accomplished to be accomplished fully by man. Not so with God. The work that is to be accomplished is to be accomplished by God. We work with Him but He provides the accomplishment. Hezekiah said they are just an arm of flesh. That is the way the world thinks. And consequently that is the way the world behaves. He says we have God with us. God is the one who wins our battles. That is the difference for which Hezekiah was rewarded, respected and prospered by God.

There is a Greek word, *kosmos*, which is used most often in the New Testament for world. It means an "orderly arranged system". One of the first things that young physics students learn is the definition of work in this orderly system. I do not mean how to work hard although they perhaps need to learn that too. In the physics class a popular example employs the use of a cart moving up a hill to illustrate the definition of work. The definition consists of two terms. One is the force that you apply and the other is the distance that it moves. All that is necessary is the multiplication of those two elements together in order to determine the magnitude of the work that has been done. Everywhere in the natural world work is very simply made up of just two important requirements. But without both no work may be computed. You must have both an effort as well as an accomplishment in order for work to be done. Now, in life, you see, God is the One who provides the accomplishment. So then with this very essential recognition, it is we who provide the effort while He fulfills the outcome thus accomplishing the work.

To continue the analogy a little further, it is interesting to notice that mathematically the expression for work is just two numbers multiplied together. The first as we learned in 1Corinthians is a tiny thing. Our effort God calls insignificant. Let us imagine this in our analogy being represented by just a tiny number mathematically. Now you multiply it by what would represent God's accomplishment. The second number would be big, bigger than we can ever conceive, let us say, infinity. Now if you multiply any very small number that you might choose, representing our own seemingly insignificant effort together with infinity, the tiniest number times infinity, that would mathematically yield infinity, always. It always results in infinite perfection as long as God is the one who provides the accomplishment, that part of the equation.

So even though we are insignificant compared to what God does we are graced with importance because of the response He requires of us in order to accomplish something in our relationship with Him. Just as even the smallest number times infinity is infinite, zero times infinity is what is called in mathematical terms "indeterminate". It cannot be determined or completed. If we put nothing into our relationship with God, there is nothing accomplished. God has chosen to depend upon that contribution. That is what He asks from us, our response, **our part** in the **work** in order to achieve what He wants through us. Someone once asked Thomas A'Kempis how it was that he had been so mightily used by God and it is said that he replied,

> I can only assume that God looked down from heaven to find the smallest and most insignificant creature and seeing me he took me up and used me.

And that is what God wants from us. But you see this is where the problem lies with the influence of the world because the world does not think this way. It assumes that we are to provide the accomplishment as well as the effort. It assumes that work is done by its own power and might. When we recognize that in the Christian life it is God who provides the accomplishment even as He asks something from us, then we are able to do what He asks us to do in a fulfilling relationship. We are able to be the fellow worker that he wants us to be. One poet A.A. Rees reflected,

All In a Day's Work

> Little is much when God is in it,
> Man's busiest days not worth God's minute.
> Much is little everywhere
> If God the labor does not share;
> So work with God and nothing's lost,
> Who Works with Him does best and most;
> Work on! work on![2]

Corrie Ten Boom was in a prison camp during the time of the Nazi invasion of Europe and she spent much time there until, through God's grace, she managed to escape with her life. Following that experience she spent many years traveling around the world speaking. She related the story of her own life as well as that of many of the people she met in her travels as an opportunity to tell others about Jesus. She used it as a spring board for speaking all across the world. As a result of this ministry, she often spent a lot of time in airports, train stations, and colloquial places that people provided for her to stay during her visit. It became as one can imagine a very tiring experience for her.

On one occasion she wrote that she was so depressed after a long delay in customs trying to get to a particular location that she missed her plane and was forced to stay overnight sleeping on a couch in a ladies restroom at the airport. The next morning she boarded a plane and the plane went through a storm causing her to get air sick. She finally arrived at her destination but as she got off she discovered that there had been an earthquake there.

Eventually she made her way to the people that were to receive her. When she arrived there she found out to her dismay that they had made no arrangements for her to speak anywhere. They took her to the place that she was to stay which was in one of their homes, just a tiny little room that was not even furnished with a writing desk.

As she recalled her experience, she sat down there and the devil began to speak to her. He began to say, "It's time to hang up your harness and retire in a nice green pasture. Let someone else do the work. You've earned your reward." She said, "Yea, that's a pretty good idea." So she picked up a piece of paper and a pencil and she began to write to a friend back in Holland who had a little apartment that she had been keeping with some of her personal furniture. She wrote, "I believe the time has now come for me to work in Holland. I'm tired of all this traveling and I cannot stand to have wheels beneath me any longer. Will you arrange to have a desk, a big one, put in front of the window in my room and an easy chair, a very easy one, on the right."

She continued her story, "In my fantasy I had worked out a lovely dream of heaven on earth and me in the middle of it." It would have gone very nicely, she recalled, except that "I just happened to pick up my Bible and it flipped open to Romans chapter 10." She read, "How shall they call on Him in whom they have not believed and how shall they believe in Him in whom they have not heard." She sat down and thought for a while before she wrote,

It's not our task to give God instructions. We are to simply report for duty. I laid my Bible on my bed and picked up the pen and paper. Balancing the pad clumsily on my knee, I wrote my friend in Holland. "Forget about that last letter I wrote. I'm not coming home to Holland. I refuse to spend the rest of my life in a pasture when there are so many fields to harvest. I hope to die in the harness."[3]

That story had even more impact on me when I realized that she was almost 80 years old when she wrote it, continuing the ministry for some time after. Yes, we are to report for duty. That is all God asks, nothing more. All the accomplishment is His, but He asks one thing, report for duty. That is **our part** of **the work**.

Author and speaker Carolyn Koons once related life to white water rafting. In her humorous style she described life in terms of a series of helpless surprises as one went down a river to meet the various obstacles that came along the way. She aptly compared the challenge of trying to survive in such a frail little craft as a raft amidst a foaming furious river. The story goes something like this. Starting off in the calm of the water we shove off not realizing what is coming next. We make very casual plans for the expected journey ahead and then take up a conversation. Shortly we hear a rumble out of sight down along the way. While we continue chatting and eating we fail to recognize until we round the bend that suddenly the distant, gentle rumble has become a deafening roar. We see billowing white rapids approaching us. Two choices or perhaps reactions remain. We might wish to find the nearest spot on the shore, jump off, grab something to hold on to, and watch everybody else go by. The other is to continue plowing ahead thinking that we can fearlessly conquer the whole river and just keep on going.

She told of her own such experience on a vacation with some friends which due to poor planning ended up in a rather comical albeit very perilous conclusion in which she reflected on the final scene from the side of the bank with water dripping off of her soaked clothes and holding the remains of a deflated raft. That was all that remained of her attempt to try and manage it on her own. With new found wisdom she then recognized that she could have done things a little bit differently. The forestry service supplies maps which outline the entire river. In addition, they note each topographical detail along the way. She then recalled the special navigational instructions and helpful hints that were printed on the maps for the wary traveler or rafter. One of those little hints cautiously advises that when you are in the midst of the rapids and come upon rough water, to site a big rock and lean over into the rock because the water will come up on the rock and form a little slip that allows the raft to glide right on by. If you lean into the rock and paddle forcefully, you will go right on down smoothly and get around the uncertain rapids.

In the simplest of terms that is some of the best advice for life, to *lean into the rock and paddle hard*. The Rock, 1 Corinthians 10:4 tells us is Jesus Christ. Lean into the Rock and paddle hard. That's what God asks of us in our work. Give Him that effort. Lean on Him. Such a simple truth and yet it is rarely easy to follow. Sustaining that effort is what Christians often have a hard time doing in their experiences of the Christian life. But you know, any time God does something He always does it in a perfect way. His ways are always perfect. And when it comes to His relationship with us you would not expect anything less.

I have found that there are two things, **two requirements** actually, for maintaining a sustained effort in our work with Him. The first is passion. Now you might think this strange at first but it is passion that gives us our motivation for effort. All of us have a passion for something. I remember my dad used to have a passion for gardening. Toward the end of his life, year after year, the one thing that would keep him going was looking forward to the next spring and the coming opportunity to put out a garden. He forever had a passion for gardening. When I was a young boy, I remember that he would begin his planning in the early springtime...how many seeds and what kind he would need, how many rows, and how much more of the back yard my mom would let him dig up this year. He would have it all arranged. Every year that was his same passion. It was not work to him. It was a joy. Now I, on the other hand, never had a passion for gardening. It was purely drudgery for me. But for somebody with a passion as my father had it was not drudgery at all. That's the kind of passion which Oswald Chambers described in one of his books. He had such a special way of saying things and I believe one reason for his recognized eloquence was that he lived a lot of what he wrote and experienced much of it in his own heart. He wrote often of the Christian experience and how Jesus complemented it in such a personal way. On one occasion he wrote,

> Passion is usually taken to mean something from which human nature suffers. In reality it stands for endurance and high enthusiasm, a radiant intensity of life, life at the highest pitch all the time without any reaction.[4]

He goes on to say, "The one great passion of the saint is that the life of the Lord Jesus might be manifested in his mortal flesh." Passion, "high enthusiasm," "radiant intensity," "high pitch," that is what generates endurance. It comes out of the heart. It is that devotion, that drive, that desire for God. And where have we heard that before? Desire of the heart. You see that is the first requirement. It goes back to **our part** in the **will**. You get that right and you have gotten the first requirement for sustaining the effort in the work.

The **second requirement** is perhaps easier to see from a little illustration. When I was in college, I took a P.E.

course. It was called swimming but it really wasn't swimming. It was assumed that everybody knew how to swim pretty well. Actually, it was partly a course in water survival and included learning various techniques to survive in a situation where you might be forced to remain in the water for a lengthy time before rescue.

On one occasion the coach gathered us together to announce his plans for the next day's activities. He told us to report to the pool fully dressed in heavy clothing including shoes. We didn't quite know what he had in mind as he lined us up by the side of the pool. We were then instructed to jump in as he directed, "I want you all to stay in and tread water for 10 minutes." In reality, I am not so sure that he actually said that we *had* to tread water for 10 minutes but given the alternative it seemed the wise thing to do.

After the first minute or two I thought, "Well, this isn't too bad." After two or three minutes, "This is starting to get kind of tiring." And by the seventh or eighth minute I found myself entertaining the thought, "I wonder if it is really harder to tread water for 10 minutes or to hold your breath for 10 minutes?" As the 10 minute mark approached I was completely exhausted. With clothes and shoes that felt as if they were now cast in lead I grasped desperately for the side of the pool. Those clothes hopelessly weighted me down and treading water under those conditions drained all of my energy.

We learned that day the need to jettison that extra baggage. Likewise, in our lives we have to surrender all that stuff that holds us down. And that is the second requirement for a sustained effort in your work. We have heard this before as well. That is ***our part*** of the ***walk***.

But not surprisingly, this second requirement goes right back to the previous element in our relationship. Jesus explained it in John 15:5. He said, "I am the vine and you are the branches." It seems simple enough but there is something that we may often not realize about that verse. He emphasizes that we are to bear the fruit, even much fruit as we read beginning in verse 2. Although we can't do it by ourselves, He reiterates that it is our job. Our job is to be the one who bears the fruit. The word for bear comes from a Greek word, *phero*, which means to carry or endure or uphold. It conveys the idea of that which holds up the fruit.

When I was young there grew a big pear tree in the back yard of our house. It was a very hearty pear tree yielding lots of pears each year. It seemed as if all you had to do was watch them grow and pluck them off at the end of the season. But during the year, week after week, as the growth continued and the pears increased in size, the branches would lean over full of pears until they almost touched the ground. One wondered how they could ever hold all those pears. Yet, unyieldingly those branches would bear, hold up, the pears.

We may tend to think of bearing as just the pleasant experience where we present our attractive fruit in a big basket, but what God calls us to do is to unswervingly bear the fruit. That means we are to exemplify those branches which hold with endurance the fruit. Now of course the branches do not do it by themselves. They are tied strongly to the trunk of the tree or to the vine and that is Jesus Christ. That is what gives them the nourishment and the sustenance. But their job, their part, as Jesus commissioned is to bear the fruit.

If we think of ourselves as the ones God calls to bear the fruit, to give the effort, He will provide everything else we need. Only then will the image of the vine with the fruit be complete. Jesus instructs that the way you do it, the way you accomplish this, is to "abide in Me and I in you." (verse 4) Abiding is the tie, so close that you can't break it. Now turn back to the little illustration about treading water. Once you get rid of all those heavy clothes, all of that baggage, you then have room to put on a life vest wrapped tightly around, so tight it becomes part of you. That is Jesus Christ. Abide in me He says. That is our part.

In the nineteen fifties, Corrie Ten Boom came over to this country for the first time. She came dedicated to a ministry that God had called on her to follow. She believed in it very strongly but had very little to go on. In fact, when she arrived here she had only fifty dollars in her pocket and a one week accommodation at the YWCA in New York. That was it. In everything she depended upon God to provide, speaking engagements, provisions, money, everything. She located a friend and stayed for a time in Washington DC. Her friend took the opportunity to tell her about various things in this country that she would need to know including using the trains for travel as she would require. From this instruction she reflected with thankfulness on God's never ending care. She wrote in her broken English,[5]

> Connected with Him in his love I am more than conqueror. Without Him I am nothing. Like some railway tickets in America, I am *not good if detached.*[6]

These last words remained the motto of her life, abiding in Him.

A Relationship Complete

We have looked at three different elements now. We have looked at the *will*, the *walk*, and the *work*. We have seen that each one progressively supports the next. We cannot accomplish one without the other. God has it all planned that way. That is part of the intricate personal relationship with Him. And He has something special that He wants to give to us in each part. In the first part we see the will, that desire of the heart. And with it he has for us a preparation of the heart which brings joy, joy that only God can give. This is His special gift graciously prepared just for us.

In the walk we have seen that God asks our surrender and with it He then gives provision, full complete provision, blessings beyond what we can even imagine. And thirdly, He has something else for us and I think this is the most thrilling. In the work He asks for us to give the effort. He provides the accomplishment but what He allows us to do is to participate in His work. He allows us to be a partner in his work. How good is that! We are to be a partner in a work that God has planned to do in this world. And all He asks from us is that we respond with the effort which He in turn will make perfect.

The Text is replete with the repetition of this three part theme. Many times the Israelites drifted far from God. And with a similar three point reminder He called them back in Hezekiah's day. Soon after Hezekiah became king over Judah he sought to restore the temple worship and in particular to celebrate again the Passover. Beginning in verse 5 of 2 Chronicles 5 we read that he enthusiastically sent out messengers to invite those in all of Israel and Judah from the south to the north to join the celebration in Jerusalem.

> So they established a decree to circulate a proclamation throughout all Israel from Beersheba even to Dan, that they should come to celebrate the Passover to the Lord God of Israel at Jerusalem...

Prompted by God's instruction his earnest command and plea to the people read,

A Relationship Complete

> ...'O sons of Israel, *return* to the Lord God of Abraham, Isaac, and Israel, that He may return to those of you who escaped and are left from the hand of the kings of Assyria. And do not be like your fathers and your brothers, who were unfaithful to the Lord God of their fathers, so that He made them a horror, as you see. Now do not stiffen your neck like your fathers, but *yield* to the Lord and enter His sanctuary which He has consecrated forever, and *serve* the Lord your God, that His burning anger may turn away from you. For if you return to the Lord, your brothers and your sons will find compassion before those who led them captive, and will return to this land. For the Lord your God is gracious and compassionate, and will not turn His face away from you if you return to Him. (*italics mine*, 2 Chronicles 30:6-9)

Distinctly and specifically here was outlined the command by God to *return* and turn their hearts to Him, *yield* or surrender to the Lord, and *serve* Him. All three, the will, the walk, and the work would bring God's grace and compassion. These three were promised to once again restore God's loving face to the people. How powerful is the response on the part of the Israelites to secure the benefits of God's blessings. But how sad that the answer to this call by many of the people of Israel already decimated by the merciless conquering Assyrians was to laugh and mock the messengers and the king. How sad today when we as believers reject this same call from the Lord. But how refreshing and satisfying when we obey with gladness and renew our determination to do all three of them.

Often it is easy to see our own nature in a child, more easily so then in an adult. Let me take you back to a few little illustrations not so unfamiliar for those who relate to children. The first illustration displays the first part of our nature from which God asks a response. It may be likened to a little child with inner rebellion. Pastor and Bible teacher J. Vernon McGee liked to tell the story of a disobedient little child who had been sent to sit in the corner by his mother. After a while she called to check on him and called out, "Johnny, are you sitting in the corner?" He replied, "Yes, but I'm standing up on the inside." That is the kind of unveiled rebellion, the direction towards self that represents the first part of our nature from which God asks a response. That is the ***will***.

A second illustration brings to mind a different aspect of our nature. In our house the occasional ordeal of cleaning a child's ears was serious business. They were laid down on a bed and instructed in no uncertain terms that they should remain perfectly still. "Do not move," they would be told with the most authoritative voice that could be mustered. Then a cotton swab was produced as you warned that they must remain still. "If you don't, this swab could pierce your eardrum and cause damage. You have to be completely still." Now the message that you were conveying to that child was that they must be totally submissive. You were not asking anything more. You just wanted them to be completely submissive, completely surrendered. It is part of their nature not to be, but that is the part of our nature that God asks us to surrender to Him. That is the second part.

The third part is recognized from yet another little illustration in a child's world. I think again of my own experiences and the times when I have asked children to complete a chore. In particular, I am reminded of nearly any occasion when such a directive contained the word "kitchen" together with the name of any of the children. And the reason is that they knew that it only takes about one meal with all present before the kitchen achieved a state that would qualify for Federal disaster relief. The response was automatic. They knew they were in for some really hard work.

Then came the excuses. And they had some really good ones. "It's not my turn." "It's not my job." "It's not my mess." "It's not time yet." And if none of the "not" excuses worked, then they would try, "I don't know how." And if that did not work, they would try, "I'm waiting on _____ (one of my brothers)." I would have been alert for that one because the brother they had in mind may not have even been home at the time. And finally, the last excuse came. Now you knew they were desperate. They whined pathetically, "I can't".

It is so easy to see this side of our nature in a child. As adults the only difference is that we have had twenty or thirty years to think of better excuses. But it is really the same. In order to actually accomplish what God wants, in order to respond to Him the way He wants us to, what He requires for us is to engage the brain and the muscles and actually do something. And that is exactly what we have tried to tell our children. Putting forth the effort brings out the third part of our nature. A response is required and in so doing all three come together.

The physical world reveals a similar three fold relationship. We relate in three dimensions. We think of time as past, present, and future. It is the way our physical nature is made. And spiritually we are the same way. We often think of body, soul, and spirit. God revealed Himself in three different ways, the Father, the Son, and the Holy Spirit. That is the way He manifested Himself to us. That is the way we understand Him. This is also the way we relate to Him, in each of those three ways.

So when you think about it, you see, each of three aspects or persons of God require a response. We relate to the Father as a child. And how does a child relate to the father? — with complete devotion. That is what the father wants. He wants the child's heart directed toward him. Sound familiar? He wants that *will* given to him. From the second person of God, the response that Jesus asks is complete surrender to His Lordship, total surrender. That is the way we respond to Him. That is what God wants from us. That is our part. It is our part of the *walk*. And thirdly, the Holy Spirit is what empowers us. And for this benefit to work, for it to be effective in our lives, we have to give the effort. Everything else He provides. All accomplishment is His, but we have to be willing to give the effort.

And so goes our part of the *work*. All of that fits together fully and completely as part of the relationship that God has for us.

There is one last verse which begs to be highlighted at this juncture. This verse I have underlined in my Bible for years. It is found in the book of Deuteronomy. As mentioned previously Deuteronomy means the second giving of the Law. It was given to the Israelites, to a new generation, as they were about to go into their promised land. God wanted to be certain that they had it all straight. This was their chance to start all over, get it right, and have the best possible relationship with Him. Moses was the one chosen to deliver that message to them. The writing converges in Chapter 10, verses 12 and 13.

> And now, Israel, what does the Lord your God require from you, but to fear the Lord your God, to walk in all His ways and love Him, and to serve the Lord your God with all your heart and with all your soul, and to keep the Lord's commandments and His statutes which I am commanding you today for your good?

It is almost as if God had directed him to put it all in one sentence, everything that He wanted. He wrote as a question, "And now Israel, what does the Lord your God require from you?" He went on to answer his own question in the two verses which combine to form the complete sentence. In some translations verse 13 starts with the word "and", although not found in original manuscripts. The second verse actually begins, "To keep my commandments." It refers back to verse 12 and all that comes before.

Looking at verse 12 we find the answer to the question in what follows. It says, "but to". I like the way he put it …. simply this, just this, nothing else, get it straight, this is it. Then he follows with three admonitions. The first one is, "Fear the Lord your God." Fear, in the Bible relative to God always means to reverence, to have complete devotion to Him.

Earlier in Chapter 5 of the same book we see in verse 29 that the term fear of God is related to the heart. "Oh that they had such a heart in them that they would fear Me." Those two words are forever connected together. Here again is the devotion of the heart, that desire of the heart.

The second thought here is, "to walk in all His ways and love Him." What is our part of walking? He uses the word, love. What word would better describe total submission, selflessness, or surrender than the word love? And thirdly, he says, "and to serve the Lord your God with all your heart and with all your soul." That is the effort, with everything that is in you, all your heart, all your soul, everything. Jesus emphasized or validated the same idea in Matthew 22:37 when the religious leaders asked Him, "What is the greatest commandment?" Put it all in one sentence. Jesus' short reply was, "Ye shall love the Lord your God with all your heart and your soul and your mind." It is instructive to look back to the verse from which He took His answer. It is found in Deuteronomy 6:5. Moses wrote there, "with all our heart and soul and *might* (italics mine)." Further we find twice more recorded Jesus' answer in the gospels of Mark and Luke with the addition of another little phrase, "with all your strength."

Indeed, all of your effort, everything, along with your heart, along with your soul, everything that is inside of you given to Him. Those three qualities are what He asks. What it really comes down to is our response to God. It comes down to allowing God to develop a relationship inside of us as believers, with our conscience, in that soft spot in our heart, so close that He can reach us, touch us, teach us, or speak to us at any time. That is **our part**. And when we distinguish those three things in a way in which God can reach without question, without having to explain them again to us every time, then our relationship with Him begins to really grow. I have found in my own life that there is nothing that has allowed my relationship with God to grow more than daily touching on those three simple truths. Take time each day specifically, explicitly, to ask God to show you something about your desire for Him, show you something about your surrender, and show you something about your effort. Three simple things that will make your relationship continue to grow profitably. A. W. Tozer voiced this earnest prayer,

Lord teach me to listen. The times are noisy and my ears are weary with a thousand raucous sounds which continually assault them. Give me the spirit of the boy Samuel when he said to thee, 'speak for thy servant heareth.' Let me hear thee speaking in my heart. Let me get used to the sound of thy voice that its tones may be familiar when the sounds of earth die away and the only sound will be the music of thy speaking voice.[1]

And all else of God's provision and purpose will follow as we hear His voice. That is where it all begins.

No Regrets

In his autobiography, *Just As I Am*, Billy Graham related that the most surprising thing about life was its brevity. At the time he was 78 years old having been in the ministry for over 60 years. Although he spoke of regrets in his life, he said,

> About one thing I have absolutely no regrets,... that is my commitment many years ago to accept God's calling to serve Him as an evangelist of the Gospel of Christ.[1]

I suppose that if we were at all honest, most everyone, young and old, would admit that as the years tick by we would like to reach the end of our life without regret. The older, and hopefully wiser, that one gets the more we realize what a lofty ambition that may be. We all make mistakes and deviate from God's will at times. But the Text is clear that what matters the most is that we as followers of Christ end well. As the Apostle Paul encouraged,

> Do you not know that those who run in a race all run, but only one receives the prize? Run in such a way that you may win. (1 Corinthians 9:24)

What is it that we may seek to win?

> And everyone who competes in the games exercises self-control in all things. They then do it to receive a perishable wreath, but we an imperishable. (1 Corinthians 9:25)

While others seek a perishable reward our eyes are on the imperishable crown. The Bible tells us that we will receive rewards for our faithfulness. They will be as "gold and silver and precious stones." (1 Corinthians 3:12) Notice that they were not just durable objects, ones that could survive the test of fire, but also beautiful, fitting for adornment. No iron or drab stones are mentioned. Followers of the Lord are depicted as the bride of Christ as revealed in Ephesians, Chapter 5.

In Jewish custom it was actually the groom who was honored and praised at the wedding rather than the bride. The bride was seen as an adornment of the bridegroom, "prepared as a bride adorned for her husband." (Revelation

21:2) Likewise, we are to be an adornment as the bride of Christ. The Bible also tells us that we are to receive crowns. There are 5 different ones mentioned. But the crowns will apparently not be selfishly retained by us for eternity, but rather they will be laid before the feet of our Lord. Revelation 4:10,11 describes the scene for some of the saints as they "cast their crowns before the throne, saying, Thou art worthy, O Lord to receive glory and honor and power."

> The four and twenty elders fall down before him that sat on the throne, and worship him that liveth for ever and ever, and cast their crowns before the throne, saying, Thou art worthy, O Lord, to receive glory and honour and power: for thou hast created all things, and for thy pleasure they are and were created.

Yes, we run the race and strive earnestly for the rewards, while their purpose is not for our benefit. But rather it is to adorn Him and to relinquish to Him those crowns in honor and praise at that joyful time. Jesus will be honored not in anything of ourselves but in what He has made of us.

We try so hard in our lives to give justifiable value to a multitude of different things, things that we believe to be good for this or valuable for that. We rationalize that they are worth our time or effort. But as the Bible tells us there are really only two kinds of things in this life, those that are an adornment to Christ and those that are not. This prayer of dedication was written by Ignatias,

> Teach us, good Lord, to serve Thee as Thou deservest; to give and not to count the cost; to fight and not to seek for rest; to labor and not to ask for any reward save that of knowing that we do Thy Will.

Herein is the challenge and as long as we maintain sight of God's direction ahead of us we will find it harder to be discouraged by the disappointments of life behind us. For this reason it important that our minds be readily atune to the Spirit of God.

Today most homes are filled with digital hardware of one sort or another. An explosion of consumer products now contain programmed electronics, from kitchen appliances to smartphones. We have personal computing devices of every size. Our automobiles are decked with an array of gadgets and features designed for creature comfort. Learning to use them all has become an endless exercise. Because they mostly rely on software which sequentially performs a multitude of logical actions, a small disturbance such as an interruption of power will upset the methodical marvel of technology. When this occurs the device will often lose its train of "thought" and no longer properly perform its intended purpose, sometimes wandering into endless repetition. When too far distracted from its programmed path the only solution is to "reset" the device, clearing the memory and starting anew to get it back on track. If only one could count, how many hours of my life have been spent waiting patiently for the little indicator light or display screen to finally acknowledge that its tiny robotic mind was no longer fogged and it could serve its human master once again.

We could smile at this if it were not so painfully true. But how disheartening it must be to God, our Lord and Master, when we become so distracted or dysfunctional to His gentle guiding and we require a "reset" to focus our attention, remove our preoccupations, and restart our efforts.

The Apostle Paul had every reason to look forward and not let his rearward gaze linger considering his days of the past as a zealous Jewish leader bent on the persecution of Christians. It should always remind us that what is important to God is where we are going and not where we have been. The news of Chuck Colson's death in 2012 was still another reminder of God's grace to redeem man and his failures while accomplishing His own good. Colson was the founder of Prison Fellowship, a long standing gospel ministry to inmates and their families. His conversion occurred shortly before being sentenced to a prison term himself for charges stemming from the Watergate scandal in 1974. The landscape of his world was totally changed, from the office of a successful lawyer and high profile presidential counselor to the cell of a convicted felon. He went from a somebody to a nobody in man's perception but from a nobody to a somebody in God's plan. He later recalled,

> [M]y mind began to drift back in time...to scholarships and honors earned, cases argued

and won, great decisions made from lofty government offices. My life had been the perfect success story, the great American dream fulfilled. But all at once I realized that it was not my success God had used to enable me to help those in this prison, or in hundreds of others just like it. My life of success was not what made this morning so glorious — all of my achievements meant nothing in God's economy.

No, the real legacy of my life was my biggest failure — that I was an ex-convict. My greatest humiliation — being sent to prison — was the beginning of God's greatest use of my life. He chose the one experience in which I could not glory for His glory. [2]

As one thoughtful news reporter put it as he eulogized his death, "Chuck's swift journey from the White House to a penitentiary ended a life of accomplishment — only to begin a life of significance."[3] Some may have more regrets than others but none are immune. Just as there are many who would testify that Chuck Colson's life ended with his heart's desire for God, surrendered to His call, and busy in His efforts, so can you and I. If we are in continual remembrance of the *Will*, the *Walk*, and the *Work*, there will be little time to despair over past regrets. Eternity's gate is before us and its shadow draws near.

King Solomon, for all his possessions expressed frustration with life as he poured out his heart to the reader of Ecclesiastes. Considered in many ways to be autobiographical the book focuses on the perspective of a man up in years. Chapter 12 summarizes this king's advice having lived a life with great worldly wisdom but now with the insight of divine wisdom.

> Remember also your Creator in the days of your youth... (Ecclesiastes 12:1)

What better advice could there be to avoid regrets. Seek Him early in life and make Him the desire of your heart.

For all of us, young or old, the thoughts behind these words, though simple, are not easy to practice daily. Our minds are so easily distracted by the cares and pleasures of this world. We get up each morning with good intentions and then within a few minutes find ourselves struggling just to remember what those intensions were. A well known verse from the prophet Isaiah may help. Convicted of his own insignificance, surrendered to God's service, and dedicated to serving Him (Isaiah 6:8), we find this encouragement in Chapter 40, verse 29-31,

> He gives strength to the weary, And to him who lacks might He increases power. Though youths grow weary and tired, And vigorous young men stumble badly, Yet those who wait

for the Lord Will gain new strength; They will mount up with wings like eagles, They will run and not get tired, They will walk and not become weary.

This Hebrew word for "wait" is *qavah*. It is a participle form of the verb root word and means "one who is continually waiting" or trusting or expecting, implying that one is continually doing, working, demonstrating by his action the hopeful anticipation of the Lord's promises and in so doing will be able to endure. This same word is found in Psalms 37 where the many promises that the Lord has made are described for those who have learned to listen and wait on Him.

The principle is simple. When **Our Part** becomes difficult and you grow weary, remember that our strength is in doing what is set before us on that day at that moment. In its own unique way for every individual child of God there is laid before us a daily measure. It consists of circumstances and people. We wake up to it each morning. In it are intertwined the opportunities for us to respond to God with our **will**, our **walk**, and our **work**. We are asked to recognize these three as we enter each new day and as we leave each old day behind. The Lord's own hand will remind us if we are sensitive to His touch.

Notes

Chapter 1. A Soft Touch

1. John D. McGervey and Bill Sones in Buffalo (N.Y.) News Magazine, quoted in Readers Digest, May 1996, p. 91

2. A.W. Tozer, *I Call it Heresy*, from *The Best of Tozer, Book Two*, compiled by Warren Wiersbe, Christian Publications, 1995, p. 182.

3. Ibid, p. 19.

Chapter 2. I Will

1. J. Vernon McGee, *Thru the Bible, Volume II*, Thomas Nelson Publishers, 1982, p. 685.

2. Ravi Zacharias, *Can Man Live Without God*, Word Publishing, 1994, p. 86.

3. Tim Hansel, *When I relax I Feel Guilty*, Chariot Family Publishers, (David Cook Publishing), 1979, p. 146,147.

Chapter 3. Not a Cake Walk

1. Ela Wheeler Wilcox, *The Winds of Fate*, from *The Best Loved Poems of the American People*, Doubleday, 1936, p. 364.

2. Charles Swindoll, *Intimacy with God*, Word Publishing, 1996, p. 73.

3. Charles Swindoll, *Living Above the Level of Mediocrity*, Word Books Publisher, 1987, p. 47.

4. Jim Elliot, *The Journals of Jim Elliot*, edited by Elisabeth Elliot, Fleming H. Revel, division of Baker Book House Company, 1978, p. 18.

5. Ibid, p. 174.

6. A.W. Tozer, *The Pursuit of God*, Christian Publications, 1982, p. 31.

Chapter 4. All in a Day's Work

1. Joseph Stowell, *Perilous Pursuits,* Moody Press, 1994, p. 169.

2. From the *Record of Christian work,* Edited by W. R. Moody, Volume 35, The Record of Christian Work Co., East Northfield. Mass., 1916. P. 230.

3. Corrie ten Boom, *Tramp for the Lord,* Christian Literature Crusade, 1974, p. 137-140.

4. Oswald Chambers, *God's Workmanship,* from *Oswald Chambers: The Best from All His Books*, Harry Verploch, ed., Nelson, 1987, p. 233.

5. Corrie ten Boom, *Not Good if Detached,* Christian Literature Crusade, 1957, p. 12-18.

6. Ibid, p. 11.

Chapter 5. A Relationship Complete

1. A.W. Tozer, *The Pursuit of God*, Christian Publications, 1982, p. 82,83.

Chapter 6. No Regrets

1. Billy Graham, *Just As I Am*, HarperCollins, 1997, p. 724.

2. Charles Colson, *Loving God*, HarperCollins, 1996, p. 24.

3. Michael Gerson, *The Washington Post, WP Opinions*, April 22, 2012.

About The Author

Dr. Paul Ashley has served as a pastor and has taught courses in Bible science, Bible history, and church history as well as Jewish culture, having been a student and teacher of the Text for over 30 years. He has been a frequent speaker on these subjects across the U.S.

He is also a distinguished internationally known scientist with over 35 years of service including Deputy Director of a research laboratory for missile development. He has authored over 200 publications and presentations as well as numerous patents. He is a graduate of Baylor University (BS 1974) and Washington University (MA 1976, MS 1977, and D.Sc. 1978).

Made in the USA
Charleston, SC
30 June 2013